was so crazy in Alabama

bearing
witness

*not so crazy in Alabama

bearing
witness

Carla
Thompson

B
Thompson

Bearing Witness: not so crazy in Alabama
© 2005 by Carla Thompson

Published by
August Press, LLC
Newport News, VA

9 8 7 6 5 4 3 2

Special discounts on bulk orders are available. For more information, contact August Press at 800-268-4338 or cwrite@earthlink.net.

All rights reserved. No part of this book may be reproduced in any form or by an electronic or mechanical means, including information storage and retrieval systems, without permission in writing from the publisher, except by a reviewer who may quote brief passages in a review.

Cover design by Jeff Harkness
Interior design & typesetting by Liz Tufte, Folio Bookworks
Editing by Sid Korpi, Proof Positive

Publisher's Cataloguing-in-Publication Data

Thompson, Carla.
  Bearing witness : not so crazy in Alabama / Carla Thompson. — Newport News, VA : August Press, 2005.

      p. ; cm.
      ISBN-13: 978-0-9635720-8-0 (pbk.)
      ISBN-10: 0-9635720-8-3 (pbk.)

1. Thompson, Carla. 2. African American women college teachers—Alabama—Montgomery—Biography. 3. African American women—Alabama—Montgomery—Biography. 4. Montgomery (Ala.)—Social conditions—20th century. 5. Autobiography—African American authors. I. Title.

E185.97.T567456 2005
305.896/073076147   0505

Printed in Canada

J.V. FLETCHER LIBRARY
50 MAIN STREET
WESTFORD, MA 01886
TEL: 692-5555

MAY 0 2 2005

About the Author

Carla Thompson is an award-winning freelance writer living in New York City. She's hard at work on a novel, tentatively titled, *The Names Have Been Changed*, about a hapless Hollywood hopeful.

Inquiring minds who want to know more, visit Carla's website at www.cwritesabook.com.

Acknowledgments

For a girl (okay, woman) who has always dreamed of wearing an expensive gown while accepting a big gold statue, it's odd that now, when the time has come to really give thanks to the "little people" who have had a big impact on my life, I am at a loss for words.

Don't believe it for one minute.

I've been waiting for this opportunity since birth.

I'd like to thank the woman who gave birth to me (in every way you can imagine), my mother, Ruby Thompson, a perennial good sport and consummate salesperson, who has supported my efforts to make this dream a reality.

There are many more with whom I have shared this vision — those who held the flashlight as I tried to find my way. Thank you all.

And thanks especially to the people of Alabama: pantheons of courage, dignity, and grace.

Contents

An Introduction

It was the winter of '97 when I landed in Montgomery, Alabama, from Los Angeles, carrying with me a few suitcases — traveling light this time, having divested myself of a great deal of the baggage that seems to be the price of living in L.A.

That winter in Alabama felt like a particularly cold one — the chill of it depositing itself deep into my bones. It seemed strange feeling so cold. I had survived worse while living in New York and Chicago, but I had never experienced a winter in Alabama before. As a small child, I spent occasional summers at my grandmother's home in downtown Montgomery. The stays were awkward because I felt conscious of my outsider (read: Northerner) status. Those visits seemed oppressively long, filled with what my young mind thought to be strange people who had a penchant for asking strange questions about my hometown, Harlem, or my religion, Catholicism.

It has been at least a couple of decades and more than seven years since that cold winter and those seemingly endless summers. I eventually warmed to my surroundings, and what was once strange became familiar. And the Montgomery, the South, that I have come to know bears little resemblance to the portraits painted by the media which are wrought with mythology about backwoods redneck bubbas and long-suffering noble negroes — too simplistic a picture for too complex a people.

I have always wanted to chronicle my stay. But how do you sum up more than five years of adventures — conversations and experiences with complicated people with layered lives from all walks of life? Although their stories are sometimes tragic, they themselves are not. In order to make sense of it all, I write. It's not an easy process, for it comes in fits and starts. But I press on.

Now, before we go any further, I'd like to let you know, or, rather, not know, one thing: the real names of the people discussed, talked about and analyzed in this book. Be not deceived, the stories you will read are true. Please. I couldn't make this stuff up if I tried. And, of course, there is more to their tales. No one wants to think that his or her life can be summed up in a few sentences, paragraphs, or chapters.

I just want to respect their privacy.

"Oh, 'privacy,'" you might say. "How would you have gotten this information if you weren't . . . nosey?" True. But my job here is to share with you a slice of the pie called life — sometimes sweet, sometimes not. I'm not trying to hide anything about me, just them. My life is an open book.

That's all I have to say. Enjoy the ride.

welcome
to C.A. . . . .

Central
Alabama

It's Broke. Please Fix It.

It has been said that every journey begins with a single step.

Who knew that my first step would be off a cliff?

The promise of my name in bright lights and a three-picture deal ended quickly after my graduation with an MFA in television production from Loyola Marymount University, aka LMU, in Los Angeles.

Working in low-level positions in Los Angeles production houses, I could catch glimpses of the rich and famous. I saw the back of Madonna's head once. Ice Cube grunted hello to me. Jeffrey Katzenberg sat at my desk to make a phone call.

Yeah, I had arrived, but I had not figured out where.

And I had car trouble. It seemed that my blue subcompact had a terminal case of whatever. I kept taking the car to the doctor, who was at a loss as to what ailed it. Its troubles may have gone undiagnosed, but one thing I knew for sure was that my ride — I use the term loosely because I wasn't going anywhere much in that thing — had a voracious appetite for money, for it completely devoured nearly all of my funds.

The darling also had a propensity to overheat during the morning rush hour. I constantly had to pull over to the side of the road, turn off the engine, and allow it to cool down a bit.

The car wasn't the only one getting overheated.

One day on my way to work, I began to sense we were nearing the end of our road together. I was trying to drive up a hill. I put my foot to the floor. The car nearly stood still, creeping along inch by inch — a long line of cars forming behind me.

Then it died. Had enough, I guess. It cost me an arm and a leg to have it towed, and the mechanic pronounced it dead on arrival. So, I had to rent a car, which cost me more money and gave me more problems.

And if that weren't enough to make my hair fall out in clumps, creditors were hounding me.

I had maxed out my credit cards making two shorts videos — requirements for the program. The indie producers and directors did it, why not me? They took the big risk and it equaled a big payoff.

Yes, I do have a tendency to believe in fairy tales. I'm still looking for my glass slippers.

They should be around here somewhere.

If you find them, please let me know; there is a party I have to go to.

They, the creditors, did not believe me when I said I didn't have the money and that if I had money, they would be the first in line to get some. They didn't care and proceeded to threaten me with bad credit ratings and wage garnishings.

"Read my lips. I am broke," I wanted to say.

The calmer I was, the more hysterical they became. It was as if they were going to come through the phone and personally whip my ass for being so irresponsible.

Sorry guys, I beat you to it.

Bad choices. Bad jobs. I once worked as an extras casting assistant for a movie about a young woman forced to fund her education by stripping.

We had to audition the extra strippers, the ones in the background and on the sidelines. My job was to play the music.

Really, it was to press play on the boom box and let them

go at it, giving us their best rendition of classic hoochie mama. I kept thinking as I watched the young women, some single mothers, do amazing and unsightly things with their butt cheeks and other body parts: What was a nice Catholic girl like me working on a film like this?

I did befriend one of the strippers, a tall, thin, half-Korean, half-black gal who looked one hundred-percent black and far too classy to be a stripper. She was different from the rest. She shook her ass like it meant something.

After appearing in the film, she wanted to get out of the game, go legit. Instead of twirling around a pole, she carried around a mop — cleaning houses to earn money and getting jobs as an extra — with her clothes on.

I got to know her while attending church. I looked around one Sunday and there she was up front, hands raised, praising her Lord.

I know what you are thinking. Might I remind you, he/ she who is without sin . . . you know the rest.

She offered to cook me an authentic Korean meal — an offer I couldn't refuse. My shelves were bare and refrigerator empty. I had taken to eating beans and grits for breakfast, lunch, and dinner. She whipped up some kim chee — a foul-looking but great-tasting pickled concoction — marinated beef strips, and rice. I thought I had died and gone to heaven.

Despite the occasional sumptuous meal, life in L.A. began to resemble that other place — the one down under, and I am not talking about Australia.

Mounting debt and a busted vehicle led me to realize that I could no longer live in L.A. My mother, who in my last days of sun and sand, was helping to fund my very existence, had returned home to Montgomery, Alabama, from Harlem. She had retired from the U.S. Postal Service after thirty-two years, built a home, a three-bedroom affair, and invited me to come and stay with her awhile until I regrouped.

As much as I didn't want to do it, I set my sights on Alabama.

I had some not-too-pleasant memories of Montgomery.

The heat. The bugs.

The bugs. The heat.

Oh, hell, I told myself, it would be an adventure. More fodder for more stories. I lived in L.A. long enough to know how to put a good spin on things.

Believe it or not, I needed money in order to leave. I couldn't very well walk to Alabama. So, I placed ads at work and in the local Penny Saver. Sold the refrigerator, microwave, futon, coffee table, end tables, and lamps — all the stuff I had acquired over four years.

I packed up all I could afford to send via UPS, leaving the rest to bless some other tortured soul.

There were the goodbyes. There weren't many. A couple of calls to some friends. I contacted my mentor and professor, Howard, to let him know I was leaving and that I would need a letter of recommendation. I called teachers, David and Marilyn, to request theirs as well. All willingly obliged.

Recommendations for what? Teaching. Don't say it.

Those who can do. Those who can't . . .

I began to think I had been cursed by the guy who set me to thinking of this to begin with.

I met him at school. He kept following me like some stalker. Wherever I went — to the editing bay, the basement, the control room, in the hallway near the professors' offices, there he was — lurking. Thin, gangly frame. Tussled brown hair. Nervous smile. Always there. Always asking me the same question . . .

"Have you ever thought about teaching?"

He must be joking, I thought.

I didn't travel 4,000 miles across country, leave my beloved Harlem, give up my hard-won, dirt-cheap apartment (Where can you live in NYC for under two hundred fifty dollars a month except in a cardboard box?), get stuck in endless traffic jams, breathe black air, and suffer through an earthquake TO TEACH!

So whatever in the world gave that clown, aka Professor So-and-So, the idea that I wanted to be in the classroom of all things — standing behind a podium or sitting behind some desk, pontificating to a group of obnoxious eighteen-to twenty-somethings. I remember how I was at that age. Smart ass. Thinking I was doing my professors a favor by showing up. Trying to get a good grade by doing the least amount of work possible. Praying for a B, C, and then, really lowering my standards, a D. If they were giving out X's, I would have been praying for those, too. When it was all said and done, I survived my undergraduate career at Northwestern University with a B-average.

Real proof that there is a God.

No. No. No. How could this guy have said such a thing? I was going to be the next Spike Lee — write screenplays, produce films, work the Hollywood scene.

At the time, I was winding down my days at LMU, working on my thesis, proud that I had successfully transformed myself into a wiser, older graduate student.

Grad school was fun but no frolic.

There was one last hoop to jump through, one more hurdle to traverse.

Production students were required to screen their work in rough form — complete with bad edits and sound glitches — before an audience of peers and professors. The screening goes something like this: The lights go out. You sit scrunched down in your seat, eyes closed, praying and hoping no one will notice the mistakes and will realize the tremendous effort you put into your masterpiece, which, incidentally, cost you an arm and both legs. Time moves at a slow crawl. You listen for a response, any response. Less-than-thunderous applause erupts. The lights go up. You open your eyes, get up and walk to the front of the screening room/auditorium and stand before them to take your medicine, one heaping, nasty spoonful at a time.

My thesis was met with the usual petty criticism at the

rough-cut screening. I smiled, but I wasn't happy. I did what was thought impossible, by friends and faculty alike — shot a film in one day in one hundred-plus-degree weather using mostly children, a Barbie doll, and her car. And everyone had a delightful time, except for Barbie, who was a bit worn out from the experience.

When finished, my video was met with generally good reviews. I hoped to use it as a calling card — a stepping stone to bigger and better things.

I was going to take on the world, make my mark in it.

How dare he? Was he trying to say that I didn't have the goods to make it?

I don't remember his name, John? Paul? Maybe George? Could be Ringo for all I know. Who knows? Tall, skinny pain in the ass was what he was. It's funny; I remember professors Art, Marilyn, John E., Sue, even my mentor Howard, but not his name.

My last full day in L.A., Howard and I met at a coffeehouse near the marina. The sun was shining; the air, surprisingly breathable. We sat on stools by the window overlooking the parking lot.

I ordered a pastry but couldn't eat it. He ordered a coffee and drank half.

There wasn't much to say.

He handed me a rock and a card. Parting gifts. The rock was smooth and gray, paperweight size, and cold to the touch. The card had a picture of a field with a swath of clearing meeting a dark blue sky at the horizon with the words: "Never Doubt the Path You have Chosen" written among the clouds. On the inside, Howard wrote: "Carla, your journey will lead you to where you want to go . . . There are many voices waiting to be heard — and they will be through the stories you tell. Best Always, Howard."

I still have that card.

I gave him a hug and promised to keep in touch. And I drove off in my rented car.

When I got ready to leave for Alabama the next morning, I dragged the suitcases into the apartment hallway and shut the door behind me. I wasn't sad, just disappointed and ready to get on with it.

I dropped off the rental car and boarded a plane to 'Bama. I slept the entire way.

When I did awake, the plane was touching down in Alabama.

Carrying back-breaking luggage, I stumbled through the terminal thinking: what was I doing? I hate this place. No amount of spin was going to change it.

I looked for my mother. I saw her in the horizon. She was smiling — probably thinking about all the money she was going to save by having me live with her. Next to her was a little boy whom I had never seen before — a cute tike of about five with chocolate bar-brown skin, close-cropped hair, and long eyelashes. He turned out to be my cousin, the grandson of my uncle who was also there.

I gave my mother and uncle a hug, and patted the little boy on the head. Although I would never admit it in public, I was actually happy to see them.

The airport was the same. Small like I remembered it. There was only one carousel in the baggage claim area and my luggage came quickly. My tiny five-feet-two-inch tall, one hundred eight-pound mother who thinks she's Superwoman (Who am I to say she's not?) insisted on retrieving the luggage from the carousel because she didn't want me, who bested her by at least two inches and fifteen . . . okay twenty pounds, to hurt myself.

All the while, my little cousin chatted away. For him, a trip to the airport was the quintessential fun time.

I remember those days.

I didn't say much. Too numb. And cold. I had contracted the flu prior to my California exit. I was in bed drinking soup when I wasn't packing. By the time I arrived in Alabama, I was sicker than ten dogs — head clogged, coughing up a storm, barely able to breathe. All I wanted to do was to lie down and feel sorry for myself.

We tossed the luggage in the back of my uncle's car and drove away from the airport.

Montgomery is supposed to be a city, but it looks more like one big sprawling suburb, connected or rather, disconnected by interstates and roads that seem to go in a circle.

As we headed towards what was to be my new "home," my cousin talking about things that seem to entertain five-year-olds like cartoons (And by the way, they entertain thirty-somethings as well.), I was wondering if there were some way to undo the child locks on the doors.

Since there was no chance of throwing myself onto the interstate, I decided to enjoy the ride.

It was nice not having to drive.

Now, it may sound like I am obsessed about cars and driving. You're right.

And now it's time for another in the series of L.A. car stories.

Let me tell you about her — that bitch I drove in L.A. — my bright red Ford Escort that always attracted the wrong kind of attention . . . like that of the L.A.P.D.

The L.A.P.D.

I bought a shirt on Venice Beach which read "L.A.P.D. They Treat You Like King" during a visit to L.A. a couple of months after the riots, or "uprising." When I arrived in L.A., I was expecting an armed camp, desolation, and destruction akin to Vietnam. No, Armageddon had not occurred. Yeah, there were some burnt-out buildings. To me, South Central looked like the South Bronx.

I never wore that shirt in public. I may be foolish, but I'm no fool.

The L.A.P.D. They had a penchant for pulling me over for the most minor infraction.

There was no justice, and I got no peace.

Okay, I was driving around on expired tags. And yeah, I

ran a red light and a stop sign. But I have legitimate reasons for all of these things.

The expired tag thing. Well, you know they have that awful, pain-in-the-ass smog check law and the DMV won't issue you new tags until you get your emissions tested. Who has the time?

The cops had the nerve to stop me right in front of my apartment on that one.

I had so much bad luck with the cops in L.A., you would have thought I was . . . Rodney King.

They were nice and gave me what amounted to a fix-it ticket. I guess I was really polite because the officer thanked me.

And that red light incident. I was driving along in that broken down blue box you met at the outset of my story. Poor baby was on its last legs. (I guess I can't blame everything on the red car.) I was on my way to work and was about to approach an intersection. The light had been yellow for some time and I was certain that, in a matter of nanoseconds, it would turn red. I had to make a quick decision. Do I stop and risk the chance of the car never starting again, or do I just slide through the red light? I decided to slide through the red light. And the cops, whom I did not notice were behind me, decided to give me a ticket. Isn't there a driveby happening somewhere?

I explained my predicament to the officer, but he gave me a ticket anyway.

Oh, by the way, the smart aleck car did start again.

And that stop sign. I was new to my L.A. neighborhood and had never bothered to notice a stop sign at the end of my street. So, I was just going along on my way to class one evening when from out of nowhere, sneaking up behind me, red lights flashing, was the Airport Police — I lived within spitting distance from LAX. I wasn't sure if they were affiliated with L.A.P.D., but a cop is a cop.

I pulled into a nearby strip mall parking lot, leapt out of the car and met them — a couple of not-too-menacing, regular-looking white guys — halfway.

"May I see your license?" asked Officer Frick.

I opened my wallet and started rummaging through it. No California license.

"I have a New York license," I said as I pulled it out and showed it to them.

They gave the license a once over and handed it back to me.

"You ran the stop sign," said Officer Frack, giving me his best monotone police voice.

"I didn't see the stop sign. I just moved into the building. I go to LMU," I yammered.

"You know you have to come to a complete stop here, not like in NY," said Officer Frick.

Was that supposed to be a joke? I gave them a half smile just in case it was.

"So you go to LMU. What are you studying?" asked Officer Frack. Or was it Officer Frick?

"Television production," I said.

"Oh that's nice. Hope you won't be like those people on Channel 9 News. I hate Channel 9 News," said Officer Frick. Officer Frack nodded.

I smiled, "No, I won't."

I didn't bother to explain that I was studying television production and not broadcast journalism.

From the smirks on their faces, they apparently found me quite amusing.

"Okay you can go," said Officers Frick and Frack as they walked towards their vehicle.

The end result? No ticket. Thank God.

Well, it sounds like I'm making excuses, but I'm not.

As I had told you, the blue car died. And that red car . . . its natural parents came and took it away. One morning, I went downstairs to my apartment's parking structure and it was gone. No goodbye, nothing.

Yes, it was nice not having to drive. I rode the bus in L.A. once. It was a funky experience. Not the fun, good kind either.

14

I rarely saw a bus in Montgomery or people waiting for a bus. After all of the historic hoopla over where one sits on the bus, the service is virtually nonexistent, only kept alive for sentimental reasons.

I even missed the NYC subway. I never thought I would use the words, "miss" and "subway" in the same sentence. I hated the subway. I would rather take the bus for hours than the subway for a few minutes. It's so claustrophobic and the escape routes are few.

I guess it was the incident with the crazy, or shall I say, emotionally incapacitated man who chased me from car to car that turned me against the system. Or maybe it was the time when the man in a nice business suit pressed his hot love thang against my back during the rush hour crunch without so much as a "Hey, baby can I have your number?" that finally did it for me.

By the way, a sharp elbow to the midsection and a pointed heel to his foot took care of his love jones.

Since I got along fine traveling on the buses and subways, I didn't learn to drive until I was, shall I say, in my mid-to-late twenties.

Traveling along the roads of L.A. gave me tremendous confidence in my ability to find my way after being lost, which came in handy in Montgomery. The streets are confusing, and there is no handy fold-out guide with detailed maps to help you get around.

And don't bother asking the locals for the directions.

For example, you might want to inquire about the location of the Wal-Mart. There are two Super Wal-Marts in Montgomery. If you ask a local how to get there, you might get this response: "There's one on the bypass."

That's it. That's all that they will say. You were expecting more?

So you go looking for this, street, road, trail, called "the bypass."

You won't find it.

The Wal-Mart he/she is referring to is on East Boulevard. East Boulevard, West Boulevard, North and South Boulevard, all comprise what locals call "the bypass." It took me at least a year to figure out that one.

If they direct you to the other Wal-Mart, they might say, "It's on Atlanta Highway."

Atlanta Highway is a real street that, once upon a time, oh so very long ago, actually led to the city of Atlanta. It's a very long street, so naturally you might inquire about a cross street perhaps. Forget it. They know of no such thing.

Once again, they might tell you, "It's by the Steak and Shake."

Well yes, there is a Steak and Shake near the Wal-Mart, but that depends on what direction you are coming from.

Don't try going downtown. My first adventure into historic downtown Montgomery was not life-affirming but life-threatening.

Since my mother's favorite saying is, "God helps those who help themselves," I knew I needed to find gainful employment. She doesn't take too kindly to people lounging about, leaving butt prints on her leather sofa.

So I decided to go to the city's personnel office, which was located downtown in City Hall. I was told by a local it was on located Perry Street. By this time, I knew not to ask for more details because I wasn't going to get any. I looked up the address in the phone book and found a building number.

I was off to find Perry Street. I had a new car — a brand new 1992 Subaru Legacy — the only car I ever loved. It was a well-worn beauty, whose blue coat bore a regal air. She wasn't a high maintenance gal, although she had an arthritic right axle. She didn't have a name. I only say "she" because I liked the idea of two cool gals traveling the road together, both with a few miles under their hoods but none the worse for the wear.

I could go on about her forever.

Anyway . . . I took the streets and not the interstate, thinking that if I got lost, I could wander around until I found my way back home.

The only thing I remembered about downtown was Ripley Street where my mother grew up. I asked her about Perry Street. She was no help either — having developed some kind of amnesia about her hometown. All she knew was that High Street intersected with Ripley and well, I should find it from there.

So, I took High Street, a very bumpy, too-narrow, two-way street to Ripley. At the corner of Ripley and High was the grocery store where, as a child, I used to buy penny candy and pickles. My grandmother's house had been demolished years ago to make way for a playground for a local Catholic church.

I kept going. And going. Past historic markers. Jackson Street. I couldn't read the writing underneath. Upscale black folks lived on Jackson back in the day. I vaguely remember the brightly colored brick houses with colorful flowers and freshly painted porch swings. Peeling paint, rusting swings, and glassy-eyed men and women sitting on front porches are all that remain now.

Downtown is comprised mainly of government buildings which are very white — not old-fashioned white but a fluorescent white. It's as if the powers that be want to make sure you know who's in charge.

There's also an uneasy mixture of civil rights and confederate landmarks. You will find both the Civil Rights Memorial and the First White House of the Confederacy downtown. The state celebrates the birthdays' of both Martin Luther King, Jr. and Robert E. Lee on the same day.

I was getting nervous. No Perry Street. I decided to make a right turn. Why not a left? It just felt like the thing to do. I was going along and noticed a car in the distance. It looked like it was headed straight towards me. It was. The driver started blowing his horn and waving his arms. I was going the wrong way down a one-way street. I stopped. My heart was racing. I wanted to live, even if it meant living in Alabama. I stared straight ahead. He went around me yelling all the while. I made a U'e and sped away from the scene.

Since getting around Montgomery was troublesome enough, I didn't travel much outside of the city.

When traveling to rural areas, people tend to give directions using foreign words like north, south, east, and west. For a directionally challenged person like me, such instructions can be a nightmare.

If the use of "foreign" terms isn't confusing enough, you are told to go anywhere from one to five miles in said direction.

I tried running a mile when I thought I wanted to fulfill my dream of being a short-distance runner. I'd get up early every morning put on my running shoes — brand new white and green ones bought exclusively for the activity.

I did my stretching. Pulling my leg behind me trying to touch my butt. Bending over trying to touch the floor with my hands. Fingertips made it. Hands lagged behind.

And I was off. I ran briskly, wind blowing in my face. Then the run became a trot. Then it evolved into a shuffle, feet barely off the ground. By the time I reached the corner, I was walking.

Every morning, I challenged myself to go farther, past the barking dogs, down the road with large houses and expansive lawns. Finally, one morning I ran a mile without stopping.

So what's the point?

On some days, the journey seems a lot longer than on others. You just gotta keep moving.

Parts Unknown

If driving is my first beef, living in small town/suburbia is a close second.

My great disdain for the suburbs and suburban life has a genesis. It happened every four years like clockwork, not as exciting as the Olympics and less peaceful than the elections.

My relatives — my mother's sisters and their families — came to NYC, passing through on their way to or from some European country. No, they were not fashionable jet setters. Far from it. Her sisters had what I was led to believe was the good fortune to marry military men, and they and their families got to see the world courtesy of everyone's favorite uncle, Sam.

My family traveled but not to distant shores, Florida notwithstanding. We rode across the U.S., a la *National Lampoon's Family Vacation*, in a maroon station wagon — style and color selected by eight-year-old me. I wanted a purple one, but my father wouldn't oblige.

What was I thinking? That thing was as big as a boat and hot as an oven. Daddy Dearest wouldn't turn on the air conditioner because he was afraid the car would overheat. My sister and I sat on the back seat, windows rolled down, fanning like a couple of old church women. We traversed the Rockies, on our way to the Grand Canyon, at two miles per hour because my father discovered that he had fear of heights.

We also journeyed to exciting places like Wilmington, North Carolina; Detroit, Michigan; and of course, Alabama.

Back to the relatives.

Once we got the word that they were coming, under strict orders from my mother, we dusted the knicks and the knacks, corralled the dust bunnies, and scoured every surface imaginable, in an attempt to make our already-clean apartment presentable.

(Note: Upon threat of disinheritance, I am obligated to say that the following comments apply only to some of my mother's sisters.)

They never stayed long, no more than a day or so, for sleeping in a NYC apartment, especially one in Harlem, was only a slightly better than camping out in an airport terminal. To them, NYC was a sewer, an armpit, an ingrown toenail in need of a clipping.

Who invited them anyway? We should have let them sleep in the airport — on the tarmac.

Upon arrival, the select aunties and their crew walked into our apartment, noses scrunched, lips pursed, saying little as they plopped their bags down in our narrow hallway and took over our bedrooms and bathrooms. We stayed cooped up in the apartment looking at one another, looking at television, looking at one another looking at television. Not even my young cousins dared to go outside to play.

I later learned these are the same people who think that Kool-Aid-flavored daiquiris and Doritos chips with processed cheese dip are the height of dining excellence.

But you couldn't tell my mother that these folks weren't the cat's meow, the bee's knees, the bat's eyebrows. Although we lived in an apartment in a prewar building with three bedrooms, French doors, glass doorknobs, hardwood floors, and intricate moldings, it wasn't good enough for them, and ultimately, it wasn't good enough for her.

They lived in houses . . . on military bases with grass, trees, and white picket fences — quite suburbanesque — bought and paid for by my parents' tax dollars. Sounds like government housing to me. The projects are government housing, too. Would they have been so smug if they knew the comparison?

The way they made her feel and the way she made us feel as a result, caused me to hate anything and everything suburban.

To return the favor, we visited their homes when they were stateside. Yeah, the areas were quieter and the grass greener, but I was bored. There was nothing to do except ride bicycles. I could ride my bike at home.

Although I was allowed "on base," I wasn't allowed to go to the store and do other things without the special membership card. Maybe I should have devised a card for relatives who came to NYC to visit. Only card-carrying members of my club can use the bathroom, eat in the kitchen, sleep in the bedroom. One sneer or snide remark and their privileges would be revoked.

For years, dear old Mom tried find the perfect house. She went north to the Bronx, south to Brooklyn, west to New Jersey, and east to Long Island. The houses were either too old, too small, too far, the neighborhoods too rough, or the school systems too inadequate.

After years of fruitless searching, my mother decided that she wasn't going to find her dream home in NYC. She would head home, south to Montgomery.

Oh yes, she would have a house. She would be one of them — a member of the sorority of homeowners. No longer the changeling.

She talked about it all the time — the house. Showed me the blueprints like they were some kind of an ultrasound. The house was her baby all right, built from the ground up . . .

On a plantation no less.

Oh, it's true. I saw the sign as we pulled into the subdivision from the airport — "Lilyfield Plantation" right, there chiseled in cement, surrounded by brick, complete with up-lighting and freshly planted pansies.

For a moment, my heart stopped.

With the exception of the first structure, a Tara-like home with white columns, it was clear we weren't on a real plantation.

To the right was a pond with a fountain shooting water high into the air like a geyser, each drop illuminated by underwater lighting. To the left was another pond and a gazebo.

As we drove through the neighborhood, my mother, seated in the front, kept looking back to see my reaction. I believe she was hoping for a few oohs and ahhs. Didn't happen.

We turned the corner and there it was. The House. A red brick one-story deal complete with a two-car garage.

When I walked inside, I knew to take my shoes off and tread lightly on the beige carpet. How did I know? It was probably the look my mother gave me.

I noticed the wallpaper with its minute stripes and flowers. Immediately to my left was a laundry room, with a full-size washer and dryer, sink, and ironing board.

Then I entered the kitchen. It was massive with its white wooden cabinets and island where you can prepare food domestic diva style. The kitchen wasn't anything like the one in our apartment in Harlem with its fluorescent yellow walls, so small that two people couldn't move around without bumping butts.

At the far end of the room was a glass table with a perfect setting for four nonexistent people waiting for a dinner party that never takes place.

The entire house had a look-but-don't touch feel.

I was shown my bedroom. Funny, it was the same twin bed trundle I had slept in growing up — so high above the ground that I needed mountain climbing gear to get up and down. The bookshelf was the same, as was the dresser and chest of drawers.

But this house wasn't my home.

Parents claim they don't have favorites. But I knew I

wasn't my mother's favorite. The house was. I don't blame her really; a gal such as I is an acquired taste.

They say it's difficult for two women to live together under one roof. What an understatement. Try next to impossible.

I couldn't do anything right.

I used too much heat and hot water, and my mere presence didn't go with the decor. I don't see why not. Everything was brown or beige with a touch of blue or green, and given my wardrobe and skin tone, I thought I blended in rather nicely.

We also had our own personal water wars.

I was accustomed to taking long hot showers. Long, hot showers. I knew that I hit it right when my skin turned a white ashen color and was so dry it required at least a half-jar of Vaseline to remove the scales.

To keep the peace, I tried to limit the washing of my body to a prompt five minutes — way down from my usual thirty.

I didn't have much choice. I was timed.

It seems that I would just have gotten in the shower and turned the water on when I heard.

"Carla!"

"Yes?" I yelled back, allowing the water to wash over my body.

"Carla!!"

"I'm in the shower," I replied.

She knew where I was; you could hear the water running from the front yard.

"You've been in there three minutes," she said. I could just see her looking at the digital alarm clock beside her bed.

Three minutes. No way. Only two minutes left. I had to make it fast. I dispensed with my three-soap ritual: Dial, to clean and disinfect; clay soap, to get rid of any remaining impurities; and a heavily scented soap, to top it all off. I also scrubbed every inch of my body with a hard bristle brush to rid myself of dead skin.

No wonder it took me so long.

But no time for that, I thought. Although I only scrubbed

the essential parts and used two of the three soaps, I always went over my time limit.

How did I know my time was up? Waterproof watch?

No.

I'd hear: "Carla get out of the shower."

The steam wasn't good for baby's wallpaper.

Everyone loves a new baby. It gets all of the attention.

It was perfect. I was not. We were both handcrafted — I, in the womb; it, in the pages of *Architectural Digest*. If she couldn't get the child she wanted, submissive and adoring, she certainly got the house she wanted.

I hated having to play big sister to a three-bedroom house.

"Carla don't slam the drawer. Close it gently."

"Carla, pick up your feet. I don't want you to wear out the carpet."

What about me? What about how I feel?

I began to feel like I was competing with the house for my mother's affection.

In my frustration, I blurted out, "You care more about this house than you do me."

"No, I don't," she replied. Oh, so not true.

But things get older; their newness wears off. And the perfect home is no longer perfect. The thermostat breaks. Paint peels. Wood rots.

I could finally take longer showers.

It's still her favorite, but now I am a close second. I finally made peace with that house which became my home. The house on the East Side — the good side of town.

Montgomery is divided into east and west, moneyed and poor, hopeful and hopeless. The population doesn't grow, it just shifts and new communities crop up everywhere.

To create a community, you take two parts vanity, mix it with three parts fear, and add a ray of sunshine. Close your eyes and say, "If I build it, they will come." Then proceed to click your heels three times and poof — insta-community, complete with nuclear families and happy-go lucky retirees.

I could tolerate living in the 'burbs because I had made some wonderful new friends — little forest creatures — wild rabbits, shrubbery-eating deer, and those most gentle of all creatures, the green tree frogs. Precious, perfect, and bright green, they affixed themselves to anything and everything — the outdoor gas grill, the patio table and chairs, the bricks.

I wanted to pet them, but I was not going to take any chances. The warts myth might be true, and I have enough problems. Instead, I talked to them. I felt like a regular Doctor Doolittle.

"Hi there. How are you, sweeties?" I'd coo. Not waiting for an answer, I'd say, "Oh, I'm doing well, thanks."

No, I hadn't lost my mind. And I'm not going soft on the 'burbs.

My other favorite creatures were the ducks and geese that inhabited the ponds near the entrance of the subdivision.

Commit this to memory for future reference: It's their world, and you are only visiting.

For instance, most days, I was running late. I'd try my best to keep within five miles of the area's twenty mile-an-hour speed limit. I'd near the entrance, and from out of nowhere, a little duck would step off the sidewalk in front of my car, followed by what seemed to be hundreds of his friends and close relatives.

I'd apply the breaks hard. My tires skidding as I stopped. Oblivious, they'd stroll across, stopping in the middle of the road to chat or stretch their wings. Sometimes they'd turn around as if they had forgotten something back at the pond. Like what, their purse?

My bucolic surroundings were disrupted when the bulldozers came. The developers extended the street creating cul-de-sacs and erecting houses faster than you can say split level.

The Garden of Eden party was over, and my little frogs haven't been seen since.

The ducks? Still there. What did I tell you?

Feeling sorry for myself and without my frogs to keep me company, I would walk through the area, giving neighbors polite smiles as I passed.

Not many black families lived in this 'hood. I didn't feel threatened though. There was no one yelling less-than-artful uses of the N word from passing vehicles. No white sheets hanging out to dry.

The only times I was ever called a "nigger" — heavy emphasis on the last syllable — was in Evanston, Illinois; Marina del Rey, California; and Bergen County, New Jersey. — never during my visits to the South.

It's not to say that the racism doesn't exist, but in many ways blacks and whites have managed to create and maintain a peaceful coexistence.

And, I might add, in these parts, money lightens the skin.

But it seemed just when I got to know someone or, in my case, felt comfortable saying hello to him or her in the morning, he/she would leave. No one ever left Edgecombe Avenue, my Harlem neighborhood, except in an ambulance. My mother was one of the lucky ones. My father was not. Grown children did move away but some, like me, returned after college to torment their aging parents.

Still, I wasn't completely at peace with living in the suburbs. It was quiet. Too quiet. Like there was something strange lurking out there — some kind of . . . you know. I dare not say . . .

Hah! Nothing as exciting as evil would ever stop by there.

What did exist was an acute dissatisfaction, one that leads young men and women, husbands and wives with small children to separate, to divorce, and no one ever bothering to say why. More often than not, all we saw was a "For Sale" sign, and we knew.

I've never been married, so I don't know what it's like. I have an idea of what I'd like for it to be; what I'd hope for it would be.

I'd marry my perfectly imperfect man — tall, dark, and

handsome. Money, yes. Good credit, a must. He will fall madly in love with my nonexistent sense of humor, my textured thighs, petite breasts and flat, bunioned feet (Thanks Ma and Pa Thompson — Ma provided the bunion gene and Pa the flat-footed one). And every day of his natural life, he will loudly declare that I was exactly what he had been looking for his entire life.

I have come to conclude that the dissatisfaction comes when the dream fails to live up to the promise of the wedding.

To set expectations low, I've decided to get married at the city dump. Send invitations printed on the back of index cards. Register at the Dollar Store. And honeymoon at Motel 6. Can't go anywhere but up from there.

After awhile, my mother felt that it was okay to leave the two of us alone — me and the house — and take an extended trip out of town. Since I was the older of the two of us, I had to be the responsible one.

Freedom.

I spent my days skipping through the house with my shoes on and taking long showers. And I dared the house to tattle.

One day, as I was lounging about trying to figure out how I was going to explain those dead plants in the front yard (I didn't kill them intentionally, I swear.), the doorbell rang.

I went to the intercom.

"Who is it?" No answer.

The doorbell rang again.

"Who is it?" Again, no answer.

Somebody must be messing with me, I thought. Or maybe they knew what I had been doing? Naw.

I went to the front door, opened it and looked out. A little boy wearing a white bicycle helmet was pushing his bike down our driveway towards the street.

"Hey, did you ring my bell?" I asked.

He turned around, "Yes."

"Did you want something?" I asked.

He proceeded back up the driveway. As he approached, I could see he was a sweet-faced boy with pink cheeks, bright eyes, and chubby legs.

"Is your mother home?" he asked.

"No, she's out of town," I said.

He lowered his head, "Oh."

"But she'll be back soon," I said trying to sound cheery.

He looked up, "I wanted to tell her that we are moving."

"You can come back on Thursday. She will be back then and you can tell her yourself. I'm sure that she would like to see you before you go. Okay?" I said smiling hoping he would smile back. He didn't.

I had never seen the little boy before. But I had heard about him. When my mother first moved in, he came to see her, riding his tricycle, talking to her as she pulled up weeds in the yard. He'd laugh as she chased him back towards his home when he had gone too far down the road in his tricycle.

She called him her "little friend."

He was a toddler then.

He was a big boy now and about to face challenges that no child should have to.

Like so many others, his parents had divorced. Their home, his home, sold.

As he rode away, I fought back the tears.

My mother returned on Thursday, but he didn't. I forgot that children have no sense of time. A day can last a minute or an eternity.

He was gone.

Many have come and gone since.

The Family Way

I'd look into the mirror. The bathroom had pretty good lighting. Sometimes too good. I really didn't need to see every pore up close and personal. Nor did I need a full view of those fine lines forming under my eyes that seem resistant to my pleading that I am not that old.

Not wearing my glasses helped tremendously.

I don't know the last time I wore those things — cool, jet black cat-eye glasses bought from two hip gay men who made shopping for eyewear a delicious experience. I'd spent hours trying on funky frames, getting their totally honest opinions as they dished the skinny on Montgomery. When I walked out of the store, I was more than satisfied.

I liked the glasses — for a while — for they brought me a great deal of attention. But because vanity's middle name is Carla, I ditched the lenses, deciding that I looked better without them. And I really like my world better fuzzy around the edges.

But sometimes I need to look at myself in the bright light to see if I am really human and not some alien creature.

So, I'd turn my head from side to side. Two eyes. Two ears. Despite the cavernous pores, my face was not deformed. Color. The black man's version of mousy brown. Not dark enough to be a wonderfully delicious chocolately brown and not light enough to be the color of vanilla bean ice cream. Just somewhere hopelessly in between light-skinned and dark-skinned.

And now, I'd like to introduce to the skin game. The family version.

I told my mother once that there seem to be a great many very dark, dark-skinned people in Montgomery. I know it's hot, but the sun isn't that damn strong.

It wasn't an indictment, just an observation. It was as if most of the lighter skinned people hopped on a bus one day and headed out of town, fleeing the grasp of Jim Crow or his younger and meaner brother, Institutional Racism.

My mother vehemently denied this.

"Oh no," she said. "That's not true."

I was in no mood to argue with her. But I was tempted to remind her of a little story she had recounted at least 10,000 times before . . .

Back in the day, her cousin, what's her name (my mother never bothered to supply one) was sooo fair-skinned that she was treated terribly by her peers. Her loving parents, in order to spare their daughter from such torment, moved up North.

I wanted to say, "See, they did leave on a bus."

My mother has her own memories of growing up black in Montgomery taken right from the pages of Norman Rockwell, complete with a wonderful hardworking mother, doting grandmother who loved to bake and sew, and neighborhood children descending in droves to sample Granny's goodies. They were happy — going to dances, roller skating.

Oh, the joys of living in Montgomery during Jim Crow. I guess old Jim Crow was just a mere annoyance, like a piece of lint on an angora sweater.

Mother was a teenager during the bus boycott. She never felt a sense of rage or impending change despite the fact that her high school classmate, Claudette Colvin, was one of the first people to refuse to give up her seat on the bus to a white person. She remembers Claudette, not for her defiant stand, but because she was smart and wore glasses. That's it. My mother marched during the bus boycott. It was the thing to do.

And the white people were simply wonderful. She baby-sat for a lot of white families who were so gracious as to pick her up and take her home during the boycott. Life must go on, you know.

So why did she leave at age nineteen, dropping out of college without bothering to complete the semester, taking the bus to NYC where she knew no one, carrying with her only a suitcase and twenty-five dollars, and withstanding a harsh winter with little more than a thin coat and even thinner-soled shoes?

A host of reasons have been given, including combative siblings, but deep down inside she knew she could never have a real chance of succeeding in Alabama.

I guess things weren't so great after all.

The skin thing also gets in the way of her picture perfect cerebral creation.

My mother's fair-skinned, and most of the family are varying version of light brown with ruddy faces, reddish brown hair, and hazel eyes.

I never paid much attention to the shade of my skin. Black is black — light or dark and all points in between.

I had terrible acne as a preteen, teen, and twenty-something. My acne problem was far more of a concern for me other than my color. I was always trying to disguise the lumps, bumps, and scars that seemed particularly resistant to topical medication.

Without fail, some sincerely insensitive person, usually a relative, would ask me the same question, "Do you wash your face?"

I wanted to say, "No, I feel if I allow enough dirt and grime to accumulate, it might help to mask the acne." I became so neurotic that I washed my face several times a day; I am lucky I still have skin at all.

So the long and short of it is that I was not preoccupied with the skin game.

Not entirely true.

The only time I felt self-conscious was when I was around my mother's family, especially my cousins. The same people who visited every four years.

They, with their red hair and hazel eyes, received a great deal of attention. Any attention, no matter how small, was like gold to my young psyche and developing self-esteem.

It wasn't anything they said that made me feel self-conscious and sad. No one ever really says anything. They hide behind the mask of Southern Hospitality — the oft-told tale about how everyone is so very nice. Sweet even. To your face. Just don't turn around.

They were deemed prettier, my cousins. More words were spoken to them. More notice paid to their lives.

My most chocolately brown cousins, beautiful women who have been approached by modeling scouts — one an accomplished business woman and the other a pathologist — are all but invisible.

In contrast, my fair-skinned cousin, a raw-boned girl with shoulder-length auburn, naturally straight hair, gets a job with her own phone and you'd think she was promoted to CEO. She gets her own apartment and everyone helps her move, carrying boxes up several flights of stairs.

Everyone except my mother and me.

Often one of the favored ones' great accomplishments was preceded by a phone call.

"Did you hear? She got a 'good' — you fill in the blank — job, house, car husband, cat, dog, etc.?" The meaning of "good" was never defined.

I hated answering the phone. I had to for awhile. Thank God for caller ID.

Life always became more intense during holiday visits by out-of-town relatives.

Like in days past, my mother would whip herself, and me,

into a cleaning frenzy just in case they wanted to stop by for an unexpected visit.

The relatives stepped into high gear. The arrangements would begin — who would do what. Someone hosts breakfast. Another hosts lunch. And yet another will cook the big meal — barbecue during the summer, spring and fall, and a large buffet-style dinner in the winter.

There was a mad dash to prepare for the festivities. My mother spent hours deciding what to wear, combing through her walk-in closet for just the right outfit in which to sit around in someone's kitchen.

Nervously, she'd ask me, "What are you going to wear?"

My reply, "Clothes."

No fashionista, I'd open my closet door, close my eyes, extend my hand forward, and grab the nearest piece of clothing. Next, I'd go to my half-open drawers and pull whatever is sticking out through the slot. I'd give the ensemble a once over with the iron, smoothing out the major wrinkles. Forget about makeup and hair. Makeup — don't wear any. Hair, minimalist at best.

After I had dressed, the inspection began.

"Turn around. Let me see you," said Mother. She looked me up and down as I did my best slow three-sixty. She'd adjust my collar, remove some lint and smooth some errant piece of hair while I squirmed like a two-year-old.

We'd drive to the select relative's home. Make our entrance. Hugs and kisses abound. So much love.

It was an odd scene. The women sat around the kitchen table and chatted about gardening and decorating — two of my favorite subjects. Not! And there was the obligatory tour of the house and yard — showing off new plants and new purchases. The real purpose was to garner the right oohs and ahhs.

During the tour, they would take mental note of the new stuff. Weeks or perhaps, only days later, each one would complain about how she needed a new one of this or that. All of a sudden, it had become worn-out or in need of replacing with the new item seen at the last walk-through. As a result, all the sisters' homes looked hauntingly similar — each with a leather sofa, a carpet runner, and a ceramic tile kitchen floor.

The men talked about the fun stuff — politics and social issues. I wanted to sit with the guys, but I didn't feel comfortable doing so. I struck a personal compromise — I sat with the ladies for a bit, to make it look good, then I left to hang with the boys.

For my sister, visits with the relatives were quite different.

I was an only child for six years before my sister came onto the scene. Six years of blissful solitude, entertained by perfect playmates of my own creation.

My sister is well-liked, even by the relatives.

How do I know that they really like her?

Thanksgiving. It was my mother's turn to host the buffet meal. My sister and her husband decided to visit from Minneapolis to help.

No one complained too badly about the food. Determined to live to at least ninety, my mother is obsessed with healthy eating — low on sodium, low on fat, and, to some, low on taste.

The festivities were going along swimmingly — the men, in the family room watching football on the gigantic, mega TV, the women, in the kitchen talking plants and home furnishings.

The younger set, not fitting into either group, decided to go to a local restaurant to chat and grab a drink or two. They all went, including my sister. I don't know why I was left out. I remember the door shutting. At the time, I had been washing dishes and putting away food.

It was clear to me; she was in, and I was very much out.

That's okay.

My sister always has a smile on her face. She is not surly like I am. She is a little darker than I and has a reddish tint to her brown hair. My hair is jet black. And I have a broader nose and broader shoulders. Did I mention she smiled a lot? I spent most of my life mad at the world. I hated when someone asked me to smile; it just made me grimace even more.

Yeah, I was mad at the world, and I wanted the world to know it. In college, I wore a button that read, "Bury me upside down so the whole world can kiss my ass." It went well with everything.

Their love for her perplexes me. They loved her even after she became a postmodern hippie chick listening to NPR and bands with strange names and even stranger music — sitars and such. And although I am an MTV, VH-1, reality-television-watching reader of nonfiction and New Age tomes, lover of all things fashionable, if only for a season, I am still the pariah.

Sister Dear loved to pull out that nervous laugh of hers when they'd ask pointed questions like the classic one — "When are you going to have children?"

She'd laugh. They'd laugh. And the whole foolish incident would be forgotten.

When someone asked me a question, I felt compelled to answer it. And when doing so, I'd look them straight in the eye.

Want to know my thoughts about education in Alabama? Don't bother asking unless you have an hour or so to spare. Clear your schedule, this is going to take awhile. I might even give you one of the columns I wrote on education for personal viewing.

I always prided myself on being a straightforward, shoot-from-the-hip kind of gal.

My mother told me that I can't be honest all of the time.

"Yes, I can," I said. "I'll say what I have to and suffer the consequences."

Perhaps she meant that I *shouldn't* be honest all of the time. Here, in Alabama, the lie isn't really a lie but a polite and necessary distortion of the truth.

I guess I'm too smart or shall I say smart alecky, for my

own good. But outside the confines of my family gatherings — Thanksgiving, Christmas, and the occasional visit — things were different.

They loved me.

Really they did.

They? The ladies that lunch, Republicans, former Dixiecrats . . .

I really shouldn't say . . .

. . . No, really . . .

Okay, I will . . .

White people.

I always had white friends, but I was surprised by how well I was received by whites in Montgomery. They thought that I was smart, found my views interesting, and my nonaccent accent, curious.

They'd say things like, "Oh, you're from New York City. I've been to New York. I loved it. It's cleaner now," and would proceed to tell me about some Broadway show they had seen. I'd smile and we'd have a lovely, albeit superficial, conversation.

In some small way, we connected — they, to someone who was a part of the fast-paced, sophisticated world outside of Montgomery, and me, to people with whom I could share memories of home.

But I also knew that the NYC they were familiar with rested solely between 59th and 34th streets and it did not include Brooklyn, the Upper West Side, or my beloved Harlem.

Who knows if it was really "love"? Perhaps their feelings towards me were based less on the way I was or where I was from but more on the way I made them feel. I did not look at them with wanting eyes which desired correction of some past injustice.

"It's not our fault," they would tell me. "What are we to do? Why don't they just get a job, an education, marry their babies' daddies, stop drinking, stealing, drugging . . . ?"

Beats me. I'd share with them some thoughts, but solutions

are hard to come by. I asked nothing and I expected nothing except the occasional kind word.

And from many, I received not only kind words but true affection. Sometimes I felt like a part of a grand experiment to see whether class trumps race.

And the blacks in town. We were okay. I even met some cool cat artists who dreamed in color. Yeah, we were okay . . . Not entirely true. I, too, tired of the complaints.

"White people do this . . . White people always have that . . ." was all I heard.

Yes, the winds of good fortune don't always blow our way. I know this better than anyone.

At the risk of sounding like some paperback New Age guru, a sense of determination can help you can change water into wine. There was no greater example of the power of hard work and a strong clear vision than the city's favorite son, Martin Luther King, Jr.

The complaints often came in the form of whispered asides, expressed behind closed doors, in segregated settings — the private self and the public self at odds. In public, around whites, they'd smile smiles too broad, never make eye contact, and speak in voices a bit too cheery.

I may find the behavior annoying but what I find truly reprehensible is the lack of respect that most blacks afford one another. You don't have to kiss my ass, unless requested to do so. All I ask is to be shown the same amount of deference and respect given to those persons whom you claim to disdain.

I have an example for you. I was waiting in line at a mall vendor when a young black female worker took a white person's order before mine although I was first in line. I stood there, dumbfounded. I kept waiting and waiting to be served. Finally, someone took my order.

In a previous incarnation, I might have said, or perhaps, thrown something. I know I didn't have to take such "abuse" but I really wanted that pretzel.

There's more.

When I worked at a local cultural institution, my department secretary/receptionist, a big brown girl with sculpted hair and long fingernails, decided to impress our new supervisor, who happened to be white, by loudly asking her about a public service announcement I had written. She recommended some changes to the new supervisor who looked disinterested at best.

I was furious and wondered why she did not ask me about the copy first. I was just two cubicles down. FYI, her attempts to brown nose, pardon the pun, got her nowhere.

I did learn a few things from this young woman.

There is such a thing as regular lettuce. Translation: iceberg lettuce. Didn't know that. I guess Romaine is irregular lettuce?

Did you know that black people drink wine coolers and not wine? Once again, who knew? Does that mean that Cristal by the case is out? Somebody alert the rappers.

There seems to be black people food and white people food. Don't ask. Labels would really be helpful — something noting the appropriate race somewhere between the fat and sugar grams.

I was speechless. What does one say? "Are you fucking crazy?" No, too harsh. "You're kidding, right?" Better, but still not good. So I kept my mouth shut, put on a fake-ass-over-the-top smile and nodded, not in agreement, but in disbelief.

Unfortunately, I can't say I wasn't influenced by the prevailing lack of wisdom.

At this fine cultural institution, we were required to attend weekly staff meetings. Every Tuesday morning sometime around 8:30 a.m., the gang, a motley crew of whiners, ass kissers, lifers, the walking dead, and those who wished they were, gathered together to discuss the minutia. The heavy hitters — department heads and those deemed worthy — sat in large, comfortable chairs at a rectangular wooden table in the center of the library/conference room. Big Daddy director sat at one end, and his Number Two Gal sat at the other.

Not all of the department heads sat at this table. The heads of security and operations (maintenance and accounting) who just happen to be black, sat along the sides of the room in hard plastic chairs with the rest of the lowlies. I was the only black to grace the table, if but for a short time, when I served as acting director of public relations.

When they hired someone to fill the position, a young white female, I took my place along the periphery.

No one forced me to. I just went.

The best compliment I ever received was that I am me no matter where I am or who I am with.

My positions on issues do not change with the audience. I am a conservative and Republican who believes that conservatism can be cool and fun. It's a tough sell, I know.

Some have called me obstinate and ornery, but I cannot lead a conflicted life. Others have found my way of being quite "refreshing." But whatever you call it, it's me.

I have decided that I am not an alien.

I'm not finished with the light-skinned thing.

I was sitting in the office one day, chatting as usual with a co-worker, giving myself a respite from the mundane, leaning back in my chair, feet up on the desk, trying not to speak too loudly and definitely not laugh for I might stir the ire of the director whose office was across the hall.

We chatted, blah, blah, blah, nonsense, nonsense . . .

"You're light-skinned," she said.

"What? Where did that come from?" I said in my head. Here I was sitting across from this fair, fair-skinned, dishwater-blond white gal telling me I was light-skinned. That's a new one. It's like having a run in your pantyhose; you know it's there and would it appreciate if everyone would politely ignore it.

It was getting a little crowded. I began to wonder if there was an elephant in the room.

Another white woman, a friend, told me that she preferred my light skin color. The admission happened when I was moaning and groaning about my dull, nowhere complexion and said I wished I was very chocolately dark because I thought the look was quite sexy and very beautiful.

Her words, "I like your skin color." Then she added, "Light skin looks better."

Better than what?

I never thought whites noticed gradations in color. I just thought black was black to them. That's it. The infamous one-drop rule clearly in place.

After the disclosures, I began to feel more self-conscious than usual. Me, light-skinned? Me, belonging to an elite group of color? It made me wonder if the skin-color assignment came with all of the rights and privileges my cousins were afforded.

Well, I'll be damned. Now it kind of makes me wonder whether whites are always so gracious to me because I am "light-skinned" — the color of choice.

And by the way, I have to check the manual first, but the skin-color thing might be off limits just like some uses of the N word.

The N word. Just say it. I know you want to . . .

I really loved it when I got the chance to interview Randall Kennedy about his book *Nigger: The Strange Career of a Troublesome Word* during my short-lived career as a radio talk show host at a local university-run radio station.

In describing the book and the author to some coworkers back at the cultural institution, I used the N word. And they felt free to use the word too when expressing their thoughts — on the book, of course.

"Nigger this. Nigger that. Nigger, Nigger, Nigger," they said. I wasn't offended just bemused. I am sure it was a liberating experience for them.

How refreshing.

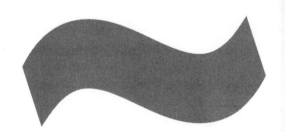

**from the
learning tree**

Head of the Class

Sharpen your pencils. Take out your books. And I'll be the one giving the dirty looks.

Work. I have nothing against it. But it seems to have something against me. I've had plenty of jobs — loved none, liked a few. The thought of working a nine-to-five job, sitting behind a desk, pretending that I'm ever so grateful, gives me a rash. I am allergic to most jobs. It's the truth; they really do make me sick.

Illness aside, I needed gainful employment. Mother Dearest was short on cash and patience. So it was back to work. But to do what? It was Alabama, and I figured it shouldn't be too hard to find something. Why they should be beating a path to my door, me with my MFA — Mighty Fine Academic degree. But they were underwhelmed by my credentials as delineated in my carefully crafted resume with all of the power words, yet, at the same time, declared me overqualified. At least no one asked me if I could type.

I had no choice but to get a teaching job. The pickings were plentiful. Although Montgomery is a small town, it has two technical/junior colleges, one liberal arts college, and five universities.

I pulled out the phone book and called university x, college y, praying to leave a message but still hoping that I could talk to a human being.

When an actual human being would answer, I'd say, "Hi, I'm Carla Thompson . . . andIwanttoknowifyouhaveanadjunctposi- tionavailableincommunications."

I had to say it all in one breath, get it out before I got too nervous and before they were tempted to hang up the phone. It worked most of the time. Thank God for Southern hospitality.

After much effort and a sore dialing finger, I finally got a gig at the liberal arts college as a visiting assistant professor of communications. One year only. They were desperate, and so was I.

The college, a bastion of liberal arts tradition, sat on a beautiful campus, an enclave in the center of town marked by green grass and early-twentieth-century stone and brick buildings. Narrow roads wound through this small campus on the old money side of town. On a warm day, you could find students sitting under trees reading or engaged in a playful game of Frisbee.

My office was on the top floor of the main building that was still in the process of being refurbished. The space had built-in bookshelves, a hardwood floor, and a large desk — a model from the good catalogue with its gold drawer handles made of real dark-stained wood and not the dreaded particle board. Everything was covered with a thin film of construction dust.

I am not a decorator — don't have the gene I guess. But I did have a plant on my desk and a couple of trinkets on the shelves, which I did fill with books — video production manuals, some of my favorite New Age tomes, and other nonfiction.

I have had other offices at other jobs. Not wanting to get too comfortable, I never bothered decorating them save a small plant on my desk. But this time for some strange reason, it was different. I wanted to create a space, a place of my own, to correct papers, to meet with students, to sit, to think. And, for a time, it served all of those purposes. I even brought in my portable CD player and played Meatloaf not too loud. Raging rock opera is good for the soul.

The students came from all over the South, mainly from the self-defined "middle class." The definitions varied. For some, middle class meant income, for others access, and for some the need to be a part of that mainstream that flowed between the purple mountain majesty and along the fruited plain.

There were very few people of color at this college with the exception of the obligatory janitor, maintenance and cafeteria crew member, and a handful of students.

I was the only full-time black faculty member the school ever had, and I was only visiting.

My students, mostly freshman, took me in stride. They liked the fact that I had lived in L.A., was from NY, and had had as many jobs as some people have hairs on their heads. Always wanting to hear more, they were happy to see a face that looked into their eyes and not over their heads.

The faculty, on the other hand, was another story.

What the students took in stride, the faculty and the administration did not. I was constantly being met by overly polite smiles and too-brisk handshakes which made my "other" status seem all the more obvious.

Why do I draw this conclusion? No one is ever that damn happy to see me.

In communications class, you do what you might expect: communicate. Class discussions were an important part of the process. Not some idle chit chat about the weather, (Although I must admit, this did happen from time to time.) but weighty conversations about the important socio-political matters of the day and, of course, other stuff.

Like things that go bump and grind in the night (or light of day).

If I have learned nothing else from living in the Bible Belt, God loves saints as well as sinners. So I surmised that if Jesus lived today, porn stars, nudie men's magazine models, and pole whirlers, would be the new Mary Magdalenes.

One of my public speaking students, Steven, was inclined to agree.

Steven was a preacher's kid, a chain-smoking bear of a guy, and a bit of a slacker. I'd usually find Steven leaning against a building after one of my classes he was supposed to have attended.

"Hey Steven. How's it going?" I'd ask as I strolled by on my way across campus.

He'd throw up a hand.

"Try to make it next class." I'd yell. He'd nod, in a James Dean kind of way.

He was a boy after my own heart, reminding me of a young Carla, who could be found in a mall or watching a juicy soap opera more than she could be found in a classroom. I just had to laugh.

He had a soft spot in his heart for these fallen women. And he decided, in this same class, to convince us of the worthiness of their efforts. Steven approached the podium and held up an issue of Playboy like it was the Good Book itself. Don't judge. Read with an open mind and maybe one other thing . . .

The boy was as serious as a heart attack. What do you say, "Amen"? "Praise the Lord"? Well, we couldn't stop laughing. Yet, I must say, the presentation was some of his best work.

And there was Missy . . .

She was a pixie little thing, blond-haired elfin girl from a Mississippi gambling town, no taller than five feet with a high pitched voice and high-octane behavior. A natural born stand-up.

I don't make such a statement lightly. I fashion myself quite the critic when it comes to comedy. I cross my funny bones across my cranium, challenging the wittiest and wackiest comic to tickle them.

When I hear a joke, I think to myself, amusing, but not funny. I might give a nod, or if they are really good, a semi-smile. You really, really have to work hard for the belly laugh. I'm a comic's worse nightmare — like amateur night at the Apollo. The audience keeps booing, and there is no man with the hook to come and rescue you.

But I believed that in Missy I had found the real deal, the next true thing. A short, white, young Richard Pryor, if you can imagine that. Now that Richard was one funny "N word." I remember listening to his albums as a kid, while my parents were out, of course, and laughing my ass off. Of course, I had to wait until my parents and sister left not only the apartment but the neighborhood. The heavy metal front door would slam. I'd press my ear against the door and hear their footsteps clanking on the cold tile hallway floor becoming more and more faint. I'd wait a couple of minutes, for my mother had a bad habit of returning to check whether she had turned off everything, left all electrical items unplugged.

Then I'd dash to the front of the apartment, pull back the heavily starched sheer lace curtains just a little, to see if they had actually gotten in the car and pulled off. Gone. And not a moment too soon.

It was show time. I dug Richard out of the bottom of the bookcase cabinets, glided him out of the album cover, oh so gently, and placed him on the record player and turned the volume . . . down and pulled up a chair to one of the speakers on the floor.

No one could tell a story like Richard with his brutal honesty; he was wonderfully self-deprecating without the whine.

I decided to be Missy's Svengali and assist her in developing her God-given talent. The class provided her with a captive audience. I dared them to go anywhere except the bathroom. They were a tough crowd — jaded, smart-ass, eighteen- and nineteen-year-olds zoned out on MTV and video games or whacked out on cherry slushies from the snack bar.

After I got the usual boring lectures (mine, of course) out of the way, it was time to begin, to get to the good stuff. I had a hint that she had the goods, but I never imagined how good.

For her first full-length speech, she decided to tell us a little story about the time she went to on open casting call for a movie filming in Mississippi. And as most stories go, things of course went from bad to worse.

It was a hot day (Surprise, surprise). Her dad was driving her to the location. On the way, she got a red Popsicle. Cherry it was. Not funny. But the Popsicle fell into her lap onto her white shorts leaving a rather telling stain in the front. You know the kind of stain. Some call it "that time," and I even heard it once called "Susie." (Really.) Well, no problem, she should have a change of clothes. Wrong.

So she gets to the location — she and her sticky red crotch. Still hot. She gets an ice cream cone from a nearby truck and it went plop, all over the front of her shirt. Oh, she's a mess. A real mess. And to top it off, she gets a funny warm feeling . . . down there. It was the real thing and there's not a tampon or a pad in sight.

It's a hot day. She's got a sticky red crotch that's about to be a warm sticky red crotch, a messy shirt and she's on an audition. She hunts down a tampon, gets one, and alas is called to do her thing.

Did she get the part? You bet she did.

And we laughed until our stomachs ached, eyes watered, and bladders contracted.

Oh, she had more. Like about her ex-con boyfriend who called her collect from prison. And his one-legged pops. Of course, this story begged the question, "Are you for real?" Yes, she was very fo' real. I wanted to pull her aside and tell her, "Sweetie, you're taking the bad boy thing a bit too far."

By this time, I got Missy to stand on top of the table for her presentation since she was too short to see over the podium. And the roar of laughter was so deafening and disturbing that a colleague trying to conduct serious academic business in an adjoining classroom would stop by frequently to reprimand us.

I saw Missy years later at a local restaurant near the school; she stopped by my table.

"Miss Thompson, we were talking about you today," she said.

All good I hoped but didn't say. She told me she was returning to Mississippi after graduation to pursue a career in . . . public relations. Too bad. I was hoping to see her on Comedy Central, right after "Chappelle's Show."

Just when I lulled myself into believing that I was a great, fantastic, perfect educator, loved by all, I was promptly smacked upside the head by reality.

I had taken a job across town at one of the city's universities, far, far away from the bucolic settings of the liberal arts college. I went from being a visiting assistant professor of communications to adjunct instructor. What's in a name anyway?

This new place was like being thrown out of a moving car on a five lane highway at eighty mph. The experience left nasty skid marks on my ass.

But it wasn't like that at first.

My first day I arrived early — way early. I arranged my papers nicely on the desk — the syllabus, and some note cards where they write their names, addresses, and other contact info and answer the question: "Why am I attending college at this time?" The answers allowed me to get inside their heads, help me plot some sort of strategy. I really don't know why I asked the question; I was just curious I guess. I did read the answers and found them most interesting. Many attended to help themselves find a better job and forge a better life for themselves and their children.

It was dark outside. I didn't know it then, but the night class option wasn't my thing. By the time evening arrived, my mental tank quickly headed towards E. But not this night, I was fueled by nervous adrenaline.

I wrote my name on the board, the name of the class, and what I wanted them to write on the three-by-five card I'd provided. I asked for the vital statistics: name, work and home telephone number, stuff like that, and the answer to the all-important question, "Why am I attending college at this time?" in other words, "What the hell am I doing here?"

I sat and waited for them to arrive. As they strolled in one by one, I handed them the materials with instructions as they took their seats. After they finished, they sat and stared at me staring at them. I kept looking at my watch, hoping time would pass a little more quickly than usual.

Finally, we began. I put on my best happy face because, darlings, it was showtime. I talked and talked, introduced myself, laid down the law, and then told the story — All About Me. I was from Harlem, lived in L.A., worked in the industry, produced and directed short films, etc. The students were fascinated and, of course, wanted to ask numerous questions but I had to cut it short. You know what they say, always leave them wanting more.

For a time, I could walk on water. Piss into the wind and tell them it was raining. I reigned supreme.

It was a veritable love affair. That is until the first test. They hated it. And said so. Most of the class failed and failed miserably. What happened? Where did I go wrong? They asked if I'd taken questions from a book. Yes, I got them from the instructor's manual but I altered them a bit. I didn't think much of it at the time.

And then they asked me if this was my first class. I said, "Yes," not remembering to clarify it wasn't my first time in the classroom. Unfortunately, I didn't mention teaching in my first day bio. Big Mistake. No backsies.

Well that did it. Bad move. They spent the rest of the semester trying to rip me a new one with their bare hands.

The changelings challenged everything I said.

"It's raining," I'd say.

"Are you sure it's raining?" one would retort.

"What makes you so sure that it's raining?" another would chime in.

They complained about everything. They whined that the tests were too long and had too many questions. Most dropped the class after the first exam. The core group that remained was meaner than the devil with a migraine.

"Why do we have to learn this?" they'd ask.

I wanted to channel my late father and shout, "Damn it, because I said so."

In a panic, I called Tom, the department head.

"Don't worry," he said. Then he added. "Did you tell them this was your first class?"

"Yes," I said sheepishly.

I could hear him shaking his head through the receiver.

"You shouldn't have done that," he said, the tsk, tsk nearly audible.

Damage done. I suffered through it. Finally, we reached a disquieting coexistence. I even gave them a pizza party during finals. Don't ask me why. I guess I am a masochistic, enabling fool.

Years later, saw one of them — the changelings — at the gym. I wanted to run but I stood my ground; she was on my turf now.

She proceeded to tell everyone within earshot, "Hey. She was my teacher. She was great."

I guess I passed.

Oh, the memories . . .

Did I tell you about Maya, the paranoid schizophrenic student I had in one my classes at the same university?

You are probably thinking what I was thinking on the first day she made that startling jaw-dropping revelation to the class during the getting-to-know-you section where I have them get up in front of the class and give a speech on one of two topics: A Day in My Life, or My Life as a _____.

No, I am not cruel. Trust me this was good for them.

Some told about their days as students — sleeping, eating, and working. Studying rarely factored into the equation. And others told of their days as parents and students trying to squeeze forty-eight hours worth of activities into twenty-four.

This exercise helped break the ice and we got to know one another on a more personal level.

Well, she got up and went to the front of the room. She

chose the second topic. "My Life as a_____." And right out of the box, without warning, not as if one would have helped, she told us she was a paranoid schizophrenic.

I'm not sure if my jaw dropped. My heart started palpitating during this "Oh My God" moment. I'm sure she continued to speak, but I know didn't hear anything else after that.

What was I to do? If I needed to give her a poor grade, would she go off on me? The only real dealings I had with the mentally ill were on the subways and buses of New York. Riding to school or work, someone was bound to get on, mumbling to him or herself or screaming at the top of his/her lungs. No one dared look in their direction. Occasionally, I caught the eye of one and became the victim of some rambling tirade. He/She would accuse me of everything under the sun, including the biggest offense of them all . . . looking at them.

I took a deep breath, smiled, and clapped at the conclusion of her speech. I think my face was stuck in a perma-smile for the remainder of that class.

As it turned out, Maya took criticism well. At one point, I told her she was a bit too loud when giving her presentations. And I am still alive to tell the tale.

Maya was one of the most pleasant, funny, and delightful people I had ever met, and she made crazy seem very cool.

It always amazed me how many students made to class regularly. And they came despite family or personal dramas and financial disasters.

College for me was a fantasy world in which I only saw people my own age. No dogs or cats even. Maybe a couple of illegally housed gold fish. No babies. No old folks. It was so surreal. I remember someone telling me at the time that those were the best years of my life because it would be the only time I would be around exclusively people of my own age.

They were wrong.

Unlike me with my piddly work study job, these students held full-time jobs to pay not only for their own but their families' expenses as well. And their names, George, Tamieka, Kelly, et al., will stay with me for an eternity. They have made me laugh on days when I felt like crying and have brought me my greatest joy and sense of purpose.

From a kindly librarian, I discovered the type of learner I am — hearing and seeing. I got information about credit reports from a young single mother and finally mustered up the nerve to look at my own. (It wasn't as bad as I had thought.) And I learned how to invest for my future retirement — which I hope is coming sooner rather than later — from an eighteen-year-old future stockbroker, whom, I might add has been investing since grade school and whose net worth is quadruple mine. Note to self — keep in touch. Potential future investor.

And I learned the true meaning of determination which is propelled by a still, small voice that tells a black single mom that education and a better future is within her grasp and a white boy from a rural Alabama town that a factory job does not have to be his future.

In the classroom, I am my most me. I expose everything I am to everyone there. I am not a sea of contradictions. I can be both black and conservative. I can love MTV and VH-1, watch "Comic View" and laugh out loud, and yet be offended by black comedy's departure from social commentary. I can have a personal relationship with God but also question the interpretation of His Word. I can be as freewheeling as the artist I hope to be and as anal as an IRS agent conducting an audit.

I can be both silly and serious. Adult and childlike. And all of those seeming disparate parts make a complete whole that is me.

Shamefully, I must admit that teaching feeds the performer, the wanna-be stage goddess in me with a captive, if not captivated, audience for seventy-five minutes.

They are at once entertained and educated. My motto is "learning does not have to be painful," which is not entirely true but sounds great and helps to calm knocking knees.

But my mission was not entirely self-serving, I wanted to give everyone an opportunity to win and feel good about themselves but not in a touchy-feely, milktoast kind of way. My goal was to provide a safe space for true communication — talking with or to, not at. I really didn't care if they learned any of the communication theories; I barely knew them before I started teaching. Theories are fine, in theory. But what they needed were tools that they could use in life.

I wanted to provide them with armor to withstand the slings and arrows of outrageous misfortune they are bound to encounter if they live long enough. I want them to remember not a theorem but that someone cared, tried to help them and did not belittle them in the process. I wanted to expose them to the range of possibilities that life has to offer, to help them understand that the world out there is much bigger than the four walls of the university, than Montgomery, than Alabama.

Sista Sista

I had had enough. We were in at war — in a battle versus the old establishment. At one point, we were holding our own, but now they were trying to force us to retreat, yet again.

It wasn't really "us" in the truest sense. Although I was enlisted to help, it really was not my war to fight. I was only supposed to be an advisor, a person to help devise the most effective and efficient way to win the war. There were other armies that tried to fight the good fight but they were handily defeated; their ranks demoralized. But this time, there was a new leader, a general, trained on the streets of San Francisco, who wasn't about give up.

The fight? To establish an integrated charter chapter of an historically black sorority at the historically white liberal arts college where I was a visiting professor. Since I was only visiting, I decided to make my stay worthwhile, if only for me and the students.

The existing sororities were none too pleased. Although it, the new sorority, was going to be a multicultural one, white, black, and Asian, it did not matter.

There were other sororities present. All white. There was a call for the establishment of a third sorority on campus.

So here I was sitting, or shall I say bouncing, along in the

General's early model Range Rover. She had it going on like that. General L., as I will call her, was a petite, chocolate-brown twenty-seven-year-old senior with a penchant for luxurious weaves and fine clothes, who, by some stroke of not-so-good luck, landed in Alabama. She had attended an historically black college, but it hadn't quite worked out. So the General transferred to the liberal arts college, thinking that this enclave on the right side of town would provide her with the education she needed to achieve her goal of becoming a doctor.

She was a student of mine. An okay student. Always late. Her gift? She worked well with others. Such a gift should not be taken too lightly. Many a playground and a boardroom could benefit from such a skill.

General L. approached me after class one day to ask if I would serve as an advisor for the would-be sorority's fledgling interest group. She convinced me that their intentions were good and that this group would be more inclusive, with a focus on service rather than silliness.

I signed on. Little did I know what I was getting myself into.

Any free time I had was vociferously consumed by pre-sorority duties. I spent more time at school than I had during my entire academic career, both graduate and undergraduate.

Late at night, the General and I slaved over a hot computer typing letters, memos, and agendas, getting punch drunk all the while. I was doing most of the typing because it wasn't among the General's skills. Loved her to death, but God forbid she should break one of her manicured nails, and what did I care about my craggy nubs.

There were also the strategy sessions held in the stale-grease-smelling snack bar with the rest of the group. We sat and chatted while eating chicken fingers, the only food I could consume and not feel too guilty about.

Bouncing along in the Range Rover, I realized I had gone

too far to turn back. The General was giving me the latest report, as she weaved in and out of traffic.

It was always something. Once again, there were delays in completing the necessary paperwork by school administration. Meetings with the administration were canceled to be rescheduled at a much later or yet-to-be determined date.

At one point, someone stole a banner soliciting the interest of the women on campus. Perhaps "stole" is too harsh. It disappeared, cut from its post. Some time later, it was mysteriously reported found by campus security who would not say who turned it in. The mysterious "they" also tore down signs and ripped them in half to prove a point and send a message.

The administration was small, thus allowing for personal contact with those in power. There was one person with whom I had a daily altercation. He was a mild-mannered family man who wanted everyone to be happy. Anyone with half a brain knows that this is impossible, for when you try to please everyone, you end up pleasing no one.

Not one to be sucked in by a smile and some soft words, I often lost my cool. During one heated moment, I said, "You think I'm a bitch, don't you?"

"No, No. Of course not," he said still smiling.

Sure, I know I can be a bitch sometimes. When I say "bitch," it is to be interpreted as a relentless, tough broad.

Sometimes, I feel it is necessary to place a well-heeled verbal foot up someone's ass in order to get results. I am not afraid to lose a shoe for a good cause.

But having lost more than a few shoes in him, I had to try a different approach since I was unable to penetrate the polite smile he would give to assure me that that we were moving forward although it felt like we were standing still.

While motoring along in the Range Rover, I decided to make a call — to the media. My instincts told me that the interest group/sorority — the uniqueness of its composition and its challenges — was a story if ever I saw one.

But like I had said before, this wasn't my fight. So, I turned to the General and asked if she would be willing to go on record.

"Yes," she said. The bold, no-nonsense mama didn't even flinch.

So, I took my cell phone out of my backpack and dialed the number. My armpits were dripping with perspiration. Thank goodness it was winter, and I had my coat on. I didn't want her to see me sweat. I placed the cell phone to my ear.

The phone kept ringing and ringing . . . .

You know. I don't even like sororities. I always thought they were rather elitist institutions whose purpose was outdated.

Well, that's my official position. Perhaps the real animosity began during my own undergraduate years.

It was freshman year at that tawny Midwestern university that fancied itself as the Harvard of the Midwest (and had T-shirts to prove it). With its lakefront views and lush green grounds, I thought it was going to be a breeze because few people from my high school knew about the school — many attending the Ivy Leagues or their sisters. And no one dared attend a school west of Pennsylvania.

No, it wasn't a breeze. More like a gust of cold, dry air.

I was trying to make the best of it in a sea of new experiences and new people. A long way from home, I relished freedom and was overwhelmed by it at the same time.

I stayed in one of the few remaining single-sex dorms on campus. It was in this fortress of femininity and virginity (That's a laugh.) with its blandly colored walls and housing project design that I became friends with a group of girls, black girls from middle class backgrounds and from states I had only passed through on one of those endless family vacations.

The girls were obsessed with the importance of status and the proper designer labels in their attempt to ascend the socioeconomic ladder.

I never believed in labels. But it really doesn't matter

whether or not you believe in labels; they are just placed on you. You turn around only to discover someone slapped "kick me" on your back.

No one said that life was fair. It just is.

The phone kept ringing and ringing . . . .

So, I was pleased that I was accepted or, shall I say, tolerated by this group of black girls at the tawny university. I grew up in an all-black neighborhood but attended predominately white schools my entire life. Most of my friends by chance, and not by choice, were white or Latino.

I thought maybe true friendship with a group of brown-skinned girls could really be possible.

We hung out in each other's rooms, talking about who was going out with whom, ordering pizza or pizza turnovers, PTs as they were called. PTs were really calzones stuffed to the gills with gooey mozzarella, and your choice of other fattening items. You could order the concoction via phone but, if you rather not have your heart attack hand delivered, you could get a PT during a late night rendezvous with the man — The Sandwich Man.

The Sandwich Man. Every night around midnight, we'd hear a bell ring alerting us that our favorite meals on wheels had arrived. The padded-looking metal truck contained all kinds of delectables. Hot and cold sandwiches, cereal, soda, and the like. All lipsmacking good.

"Sandwich Man! Sandwich Man!" we would yell gleefully as we ran about knocking on doors, scrambling to slip on slippers over stockinged feet and sweats over pajamas and gowns. Wearing baseball caps and head rags, down coats and earmuffs, we'd run out into sometimes subzero weather to meet the Man.

Thanks to our late night eatfests, we packed on the pounds. What did we care? We were having too much fun to notice.

We loved playing cards. Even played cards during finals week. I learned very little about calculus and a lot about bid whiz. And we loved our music. Luther Vandross was big. "A

House Is Not a Home" was the slow jam. Couldn't get enough of it. Prince was the rage. A friend had a poster of him in his scantily clad best on her wall.

The parties. They were sponsored by one of the three black fraternities or two black sororities on campus. The girls and I (there were about five of us) made the rounds to every single one, which were held in the basement or large common area of some dormitory. Yeah, we may not have made it to every class, but we were at every dance.

And unlike the high school dances where I held up the wall, guys actually asked me to dance.

We thought we were the shit in our nicely pressed jeans and polo shirts — the alligator was all the rage and Ralph was beginning to make a stand.

It was our own little black planet in the predominately white university whose students looked at us as if we were some affirmative action babies left on their doorstep.

Our precious world was sometimes invaded by aliens. In the whitewashed world of fraternity row with its large houses with good help, they called such intruders, "townies." Black students were far less kind to their African American counterparts — calling them, the unwanted, "cooties."

With status being so important, convincing themselves — ourselves, that we were not like those people, was a psychological necessity. We are supposed to be different. Special. So they were named — like something below the dregs of the earth, like something that one should inoculate oneself against, excavations from a nasal cavity.

But no matter how much we may have crossed our fingers and our toes, they still came.

And these "cooties" were angry. Mad has hell. Not because they knew what we called them but because they knew how we felt about them. They refused to stay in their place. So they invaded the parties, often wreaking havoc; starting fights and sometimes engaging in vandalism.

Young and ignorant, we thought we were so much more

than they were. I suspect many of those same students went home to folks that looked like "cooties" calling them perhaps, "brother," "uncle," or "cousin."

And to think some of the people I have met in Alabama, whom I might have once categorized as "undesirables," are good friends and acquaintances. They have taught my overeducated ass a thing or two.

Perhaps it's true — with age really does come wisdom.

But back then, I must admit I was not above the fray.

Just my luck a "cootie" would approach me and ask me to dance. They didn't really ask, just grunted and motioned in Neanderthal-like fashion towards the dance floor. I may have been cocky, but I wasn't crazy. Too frightened to protest, I slinked off to the dance floor dragging my feet behind me. Dead woman walking.

My girls were standing on the sidelines snickering.

The "cooties" wore the hairstyle of the day. Jheri curl. But they got a little too happy with the activator not quite understanding that less is more. No polo shirts, freshly ironed jeans, or loafers for them, only a lot of glitter and flash — like something found at a pimp's garage sale.

I tried not to look at them as we danced; I felt it was much safer that way. I didn't want them to get any ideas. And I was trying to keep from being blinded by the flying drops of activator.

They always danced wildly — flailing arms, legs jerking like they were having some terrible fit. Funky chicken gone mad. I made sure that I fled at the hint of a slow song.

I hung up . . . and dialed again . . .

Although at the tawny university I felt more confident than I had in years, I knew it was not my world. It belonged to the sorority girls.

The sorority girls got to wear special colors and make loud strange calls across the campus to one another. Just a single call could distinguish one group from another. The guys, fraternity boys, had calls, hand signals, and a special handshake. They were all sistas and brothas, members of a special group.

I've never really fit in anywhere. I thought it might be nice to belong to a group, a sorority — to be part of a club. So I went to their information sessions.

These sessions were formal affairs. High teas wherein everyone dressed up in suits and nice clothes. I had a hard time finding something to wear — the addition of the freshman fifteen to my waist, hips and derriere, limiting my choices.

I selected a sorority to join, not on the basis of any real evaluation of their offerings, I just picked the one that my friends wanted to join.

There was no real difference between the two. One wore one set of colors, the other another.

I thought that perhaps more guys would ask me to dance. They seemed to like those sorority girls better. The sistas got to dance with all the really good-looking guys.

But before I could begin the process of becoming a member, I had to get through the interview, or shall I say inquisition.

It's a very secretive process. I can share this with you because I am sure that you will not tell anyone.

Well, there I sat in a cavernous conference room, in my too-tight suit, pinching the hell out of my thick waist. In front of me, miles away, or so it seemed, was a long table behind which the sistas sat dressed in their Sunday best with the most serious looks on their faces.

They were going to make me talk, find out what I was really made of.

Yep, there I sat on a hard plastic chair with no arms while the sistas fired questions at me in rapid succession. They were strange questions which were meant to test my commitment to the ideals of true black sistahood.

"What would make you drop line?" they asked.

Let me explain "line." It's part of the initiation process. The nubies form a cohesive group which must do everything together, including walk in a straight line when in public. All for one and one for all, like some twisted Musketeers.

Well, I said, "Any threat of physical punishment, I guess."

Strike One.

These sororities are known for their disciplining techniques. Like the Armed Forces — they like to tear you down in order to build you back up. It was rumored that a little ass whipping, both verbally and physically, was to be expected. But you won't hear talk like that from any of the sistas. They'd vehemently deny any and all allegations because admitting to such would lead to sanctions which could include the revocation of their charter. (In Grandma English, it would get their sorority kicked off campus.)

Rumor or not, I wasn't going to take any chances; I wanted to make my position clear.

As I sat on that hard-ass chair, my butt growing numb, I convinced myself that the process would help me take orders more graciously. Maybe I needed a bit of practice in kowtowing.

I can be a bit confrontational. But, I don't start fights. Not physical ones. I run from those. Verbal ones. That's another story.

Okay, I thought to myself, maybe I can recover. I answered the next few questions to my satisfaction. Then came the final question.

"What was the last secret someone told you?"

"I don't remember," I said.

The correct answer would have been, "I can't tell you because it's a secret."

You could have stuck a fork in my porky butt because I was done.

I was never really good at keeping secrets. I was always compelled to reveal the information to at least one person, one trusted soul.

"Don't tell anyone, okay?" I'd say.

"Okay," they would say. Then I'd give them the story, sparing no details. I'd make them swear on their first born or favorite body part that they wouldn't tell a soul.

My friends went on to join the sorority. Many were on the academic brink before becoming members. The pledge process, which lasted several weeks and caused them to spend more time satisfying the whims of the sistas than the course requirements, sent them right over the edge into academic disaster.

We were no longer friends. They were members of the exclusive club, and I was just . . . well, me . . . no one really special or so they thought.

I was glad I was rejected. Really, I was. I got to graduate from the prestigious university in four years. It's an accomplishment that I found more satisfying than wearing colors and screaming calls.

"Hello." A real voice. I was startled.

"Hi, I'm calling on behalf of XXX (Not the real name, but wouldn't it be interesting if it were?) sorority interest group," I said. Lame, I thought. Very lame. All the venom was gone. The righteous indignation, too. What was I thinking? I was not fighting to save the free world. It was only a sorority for God's sake.

Sometimes I feel I have to get into verbal altercations to let the world know that I am serious. Like some damn Chihuahua, I bark loud and often to make sure that "they" — the much-despised, often talked about "they" — understand that my kindness should not be mistaken for weakness.

I decided that the administration is not really the face of evil. And perhaps any resistance we received was their response to some kind of deep-seated ancestral fear. We, oh, I mean, the sorority, craved to move ahead with all deliberate speed and they — the administration — wanted to take a slow approach, perhaps hoping that once again the girls' efforts would wane, for the institution was struggling to retain, attract, and appease a certain group of students that it perceived to be its bread and butter — the source of its very survival.

The girls were hopelessly caught in the middle of a struggle between the past and the future.

I handed the phone to the General who spoke to the reporter about the group. Their efforts were of no surprise to him — a relative had told him about them.

Well, so much for that.

A lot of time passed and no article. In the meantime, there were fundraisers — talent shows, fashion shows, raffles, etc. Being a sista doesn't come cheap. The General did not want anyone to be left out due to lack of money. Whatever money was raised was going to be split among them evenly. Each dollar raised, and they raised quite a few, brought them closer to their goal.

But then came a crisis.

The General informed me that there was talk of a mass defection brewing.

Oh no. Oh hell no.

I told her to call a meeting right away. A mandatory meeting. I had a few things to say.

So we met in an upstairs room of one of the academic buildings that was badly in need of repair. It smelled of rotting wood and dead things. The girls sat around in rickety chairs and on the sofas with tattered upholstery and with springs so worn out it made getting up a two-person task.

The General sat behind her desk. Before I could catch my breath from the walk up one flight of stairs, she handed the meeting over to me.

"Ms. Thompson has a few things to say to you," said General L.

Oh, okay.

I had planned what I was going to say all day. There was not going to be a defection. Not on my watch. This was war, and all hands had to be on deck.

I immediately laid into them.

"You have to take responsibility. If something is not getting done, you have to step forward to do it," I said, my voice sounding loud and strong.

I declared a no-whining zone. I didn't want to hear about

their cramps, broken nails, or pesky zits.

We, I mean, they, were fighting a battle for the life of a dream. They were doing it not only for themselves but for all of those who had come before and all of those who may come after.

And I added, "I'm giving my all, and I don't even like sororities."

Totally unnecessary, I know, but it had to be said.

They stared at me in stunned silence.

I'm not sure if I went on for five, fifteen, or fifty minutes but for them it must have felt like an eternity.

My tirade did the trick. When the General asked for volunteers for the next project, she didn't have any problems getting recruits.

Then it came out.

"It" was a cover story in the local paper complete with a picture of the racially diverse group sitting on the school's front lawn.

Of course everyone was on board after that, and had only glowing things to say. And things began to move forward rather quickly.

I got them to the door but I could not walk them through it. I was not a soror, a sista. So they were on their own from now on. I had made a decision not to return to the school the next academic year. Well, the administration made it for me. They wanted a Ph.D. not an MFA although both were terminal degrees. It could have been more than that, but it doesn't matter really.

The charter was granted. Members of the administration were sent invitations to the induction ceremony held by the local graduate chapter. I was not.

The excuse? None given.

I saw the girls, now sistas, after it was all over. They were dressed in the colors, calling to one another using their special call. I was, yet again, an outsider.

Flesh Wounds

S istahood can be that thing that binds us together, through joy or pain and knowing.

Back to the university. Final semester.

We, me and the sleep-deprived students, all came to the conclusion that 8 a.m. was far too early to think let alone speak, but we did our best. To help matters, I arrived at least twenty minutes early — not to do some extra photocopying but to try to get my juices going before class. Chatting with the department secretary and assistant dean helped sometimes. Still, I felt that I should do several jumping jacks, push ups, and run around the block before beginning the hour-and-a-half slow crawl.

Thank God they were a lively bunch. Late most of the time. Very late the rest. The motley crew which included a wanna-be saint, a librarian, and an ex-druggie, asked interesting questions, made stunning analogies, and provided an amen chorus for one another. With this class, I *really* learned to expect the unexpected.

One student, a tough gal named Tina, approached me after class one day. She wore baggy pants, sweats, a skullcap sweater hat, spoke in staccato voice with a Southern twang, and had a penchant for interjecting the word, crap, into a sentence.

"Ms. Thompson. Maybe you can help me. I want to be a motivational speaker," she said.

"Okay," I said. Now when you say "motivational speaker" I think of self-appointed, sometimes unctuous characters, cheerleaders who work you up into a frenzy and send you out into the cold all sweaty to catch pneumonia. But she was different.

She told me that she had been raped and molested. My mind quickly went to work.

"Come on. Follow me," I said.

She followed me down the hall and into the department office. I leaned over the counter.

"Diane, do you have a phone book?" I asked the department secretary.

"Maybe we can look up rape crisis center," I told Tina.

"I got a phone book in my dorm. Thank you Miss Thompson," she said.

"You're welcome. Good luck."

After she left the office, I began thinking a lot about her. Sometimes I think that I think just a little too much. The next day, I approached her before class.

"Hey, I got an idea," I said, a smile on my face.

"I want to talk to you. I have something to ask you," she said.

After class, she stood in the line that formed around my desk and waited patiently for her turn.

She approached.

Before she could get a word in I said, "Why don't you give a speech on rape and molestation. It would be a great way to practice your skills, test things out."

She was way ahead of me.

"That's what I wanted to ask you about," she said with a smile.

The day came. It was their first long-form speech and Tina was the last to go. I was more nervous than she was. I had recommended that she give the speech in the first place.

She placed a clock on the long table — a children's clock with big removable numbers. On the sill of the blackboard, she placed a poster board with family photos of good times with people posed in sets of twos and threes.

Then she wrote on the board, "One in four people is raped every six seconds."

Good start; it got our attention.

"Look at these pictures. You see people with happy faces, but you really don't know what's going on in these families behind closed doors," she said, shifting her weight, pointing to the poster.

"I was raped and molested," she said trying to be a bit off the cuff.

Deafening silence.

Overtaken by nervousness, she started rambling — her speech peppered with bits of profanity. Although I'm not a person that stands on formality, it started getting a little too real, even for me. I began to cringe.

She told us how she preferred to have male friends because she found them more compassionate and women far more judgmental. Her boyfriend was understanding, her father also. But, her mother, although she loves her, was far less so.

"I don't wear tight clothes, I dress down," she said as she tugged on her loosely-fitting, baggy white T-shirt. She didn't want to attract attention to herself.

She cautioned the group to withhold judgement of women who dressed provocatively for something else might be going on.

I sat in front and dared not look around. The usually chatty group was drop dead silent.

She went on.

She had forgiven her attacker and said that she would even give him money if he needed it. Her religion had taught her that — forgiveness. She was seeking treatment which was for her both helpful and painful; causing her to think a lot about what happened — maybe too much.

"I'm just crazy," she said with a smile.

She was doing this — opening herself up — to help others.

At the conclusion of her presentation, there were no questions from the audience. Everyone packed up his/her stuff and headed off to the next class. She seemed to take it okay. The nun wannabe did stop to chat with her afterwards. Getting in a little practice, I guess.

Yes, it was all my fault. What was I going to do? To top it all off, I had to give her a grade.

When grading speeches, I had a system. I don't know if it was the best, but it worked for me. I broke down the effort into categories: organization and preparation, vocal quality, body movement, etc., with each section/element receiving a score from one to twenty.

I didn't want to silence Tina, I just wanted her to refine her presentation, to soften but not dull the jagged edges. Fine-tune it. Make it a bit more palatable.

It was not the first time I had heard someone address this issue. In a previous semester, a student talked about her anorexia, which was brought on by an incident with a boy, a friend, who "took advantage" of her during a school trip. The young woman's tall, thin frame wasted away until she passed out one day, alerting her parents of the condition for the first time.

There were questions after the presentation about anorexia and its effects — the usual stuff about eating habits and hair loss.

But there was one very memorable question, "What would have helped you not to become anorexic?"

She said, "If someone would have believed me."

We are familiar with anorexia; we can talk about it in polite circles. And we can talk about rape in the abstract using statistics, what ifs, and awkward verbal substitutions. The difference between Tina and the girl with anorexia was that she took us in an unvarnished and bold manner and challenged our own sense of culpability. The room was silent because no one wants to give his or her two cents when the finger points directly at him or her.

It was time to grade the speeches. I went through everyone's rather quickly. Then, I came to hers, and if I had graded it on the usual scale, she would have gotten a D at best. So, I put away my notes. Sat on it for a bit to think about what to do.

Finally, I had waited — procrastinated — long enough. A good week after giving out the grades, I decided to give her handwritten comments. No grade. Everyone gets one concession during the semester, whether he/she deserves it or not.

It was a fair, although not a glowing report. Don't lean on the podium or blackboard. Use more facts. By all means, no profanity. Try to relate to the audience more.

I handed her the comments in an envelope before class. She peeked inside the envelope, then pulled out the paper and read it. I met her outside after class.

"Did you understand what I wrote?" I asked.

"Yes, thanks," she said.

She knew she had made some fatal errors.

"Don't give up. Take what happened and learn from it. For next time."

She thanked me again.

I don't know if Tina ever became a rape counselor.

Flashback to years earlier. To the liberal arts college where I learned that it's better to light a single candle.

It was raining. Spritzing spring rain — annoying in its consistency. That's all we needed. Rain. Students don't need much of an excuse not to come to class, much less an extra-curricular activity.

I entered the school's gym. Some of the lights were dim. Two young men, boyfriends of my students, were setting up the sound — boom boxes with speakers — trying to attach some wires and find available outlets.

"Everything okay?" I asked one of the boyfriends, shaking the water off of my umbrella

"Yeah."

"Good. I guess they (the girls) are still downtown," placing my stuff on a bleacher.

"Yeah."

The girls rushed in — a brown haired, petite California-cute girl and her friend, a tall, rawboned blond with a lazy walk.

"Hey, Miss Thompson."

"Hey."

"Don't stress. I got them," said the blond to the brunette as she headed toward one of boxes resting on the table.

"How was the 'Fight Against Rape' rally?" I asked.

"It was good," said the blond.

"Did a lot of people show?" I asked.

"Not really," said the brunette.

"Is there anything I can do?" I asked, feeling a bit awkward.

"No, I don't think so."

They were running late. With only minutes to go before everything was to begin, some people were starting to enter, walking gingerly as if stepping around land mines, or over chards of broken glass. I decided to act as hostess.

"Come in and sit down. Thanks for coming."

The brunette and blond were sorority girls, and some of their members came out to support their sisters' efforts.

Wearing Greek-lettered T-shirts and sweatshirts, they nervously smiled and waved.

The blond handed each of them a slender white candle.

"Just hold on to it."

They took their seats. More came — mainly women, a few men. Each receives a candle.

The lights were dimmed. The brunette lit her candle and passed her flame along to the next person. Each person did the same until all the candles were lit.

Then the ceremony began.

"Welcome to Take Back The Night: a vigil for victims of domestic violence and rape. It is a part of an assignment to create a movement on campus. It is for my class taught by Miss Thompson," announced the brunette.

It was my last stand at the liberal arts college, my visit rapidly coming to a close. That night was the culmination of endless meetings with Mr. Smiley Face, who made us promise not to generate outside publicity. "Yes," I promised. Cross my heart and hope you . . .

A representative of the rape crisis center spoke. A call for volunteers was made. They needed people to go with the women to the hospital and to the police station, to sit with them to comfort them.

And then the representative said it. She, a former student, had been a victim of date rape and somberly recounted her experience.

Finally, a poem was read. There was a solemn silence — a moment of reflection for the victims and ourselves.

I looked around at teary-eyed young women and somber young men. Nearly twenty-five were present, more than attend most events.

It was over. The lights were turned on. Candles blown out. Pamphlets distributed.

I helped them take down the table and put some things away.

The brunette and I hugged, tears streaming down our faces. We need not say anything. I knew. She knew. What had happened was far greater than a moment, bigger than a class.

I think about Tina and those young women often.

I still haven't really forgiven and I am not nearly as brave.

It's Not How You Play the Game

I looked at my watch, streams of sweat coursing down my body, 10:30.

The internal dialogue began.

"That gives me a half hour to run home. No, I can't do that. I just need to get there. If I go home, I'll start putzing around, getting something to eat, smoothing my hair, and going to the bathroom. No, I'll just cross my legs, suck on my tongue for refreshment and listen to the swishing sounds of my stomach acid. I have to get there. On time. I must redeem myself."

I had been at the gym. It was Saturday morning, and I needed to get in a real good sweat before Sunday, my day off. Even He had a day of rest. Normally, I took Sunday off, not for religious reasons. Since I spent most of my Sundays watching church instead of attending it, I didn't feel worthy to actually partake of any real pleasurable pursuits. Sounds good huh? Sounded pretty good to me, too. The real truth. I'll use any excuse to take time off, eat, and lounge around.

I was sweaty, hoping to dry on the way over. I hopped in

my car. I took Taylor Road, a four-lane thoroughfare, past the new outdoor mall, zooming along at least ten miles per above the speed limit. It was totally acceptable behavior, of course, for the speed limit expresses a range — plus or minus ten above the posted limit. Just in case a police officer might be inclined to disagreed, I looked in the rearview and side mirrors. No police.

I turned onto the university campus, zooming around the winding single lane road, traveling fifteen miles an hour over the limit. I navigated around the hump — not a speed bump but massive pothole that never gets filled, and then I turned into the parking lot. Plenty of spaces were available. I pulled into one. I looked at my watch 10:50. Perfect.

My chest pounding, I got out of the car. I looked into the distance as a figure approached. It was Diane, the department secretary. She had called me at home to tell me about the practice at 11 a.m.

"Sorry, Carla, they met at eight. I don't know what I was thinking. I went upstairs, and everything was over."

I smiled and said, "That's okay," as I turned around to go back to my car.

No, it wasn't okay. My one and only chance blown. Excuse me while I get in touch with my weeping.

It was not going to be. I was going to go down in the annals of College Bowl history as a loser — the one that blew it for the team — missed the lay-up in the last few seconds, fumbled the ball in the end zone as the clock ticked towards zero. That's me — LOSER.

As I sat in my car feeling a bit dejected, I realized that it was all Barry's fault. He was the one who invited me to College Bowl — first to observe and later to play.

College Bowl. It's like Jeopardy. Hard questions from many disciples which, unlike Jeopardy, are not answered in question form. You compete against smarties from other colleges to win glory and recognition. There are buzzers like "Jeopardy" — smooth, long, and thick like the pencils you used in first grade. There is also the dreaded time clock. Each question is worth certain number of points. If you answer toss up question correctly, you get a shot at additional bonus questions.

The team practiced because, although practice may not make perfect, it at least makes you better. We ran mock "competitions" against a tough team from the other side of town, an HBC, (Historically Black College) who was serious about kicking some College Bowl A-S-S. All of their students were members of the honors program.

We, on the other hand, scraped by with whomever was breathing and could make it to the internal practices on Friday morning. On the day of the mock competition, a faculty member usually had to play so that the group could have a quorum.

The HBC had a deep bench enabling them to make multiple substitutions. They studied the final score card to see who was performing and who was not. We didn't care about the score card. Who needs more paper?

We practiced against one another, but we did not compete on the same circuits. They were going for the big bucks, traveled to Disney World to vie for a $50,000 prize. And us, well, we just want to win a round, for once.

Barry, the leader of the group, was one of my students in "Introduction to Communication." The first day of class, he rolled in late. His excuse: the elevators were terribly slow. He was appropriately apologetic, so I wasn't mad at him.

Perhaps I should explain "rolled in" — Barry is wheelchair-bound. He was one of the many special students I had that semester, my final one.

He had CP. Has CP. Cerebral Palsy. I didn't know it at first. He was young. I thought his disability might have been the result of an accident or a shooting. It's not uncommon to see a young black man confined to a wheelchair, a victim of mean streets.

I was hoping to find out more about Barry during the first exercise — the impromptu speech exercise, My Life as a ___ ___, or A Day in My Life.

His speech was My Life as a Watch. He proceeded to tell us about his tight schedule — all of his activities were perfectly timed, scheduled down to the minute. I guess getting to class on time wasn't on his schedule.

Nosey me, of course, wanted to find out why he was in the chair.

I did not find out what I wanted to know, but I did learn a lot. Barry had a grand laugh that filled the room, a wandering eye, and some awkwardness with his hands.

But he was more than his disability. Barry, an information systems major, lived a full life which included giving speeches on disabilities, working in the office of special services, and playing wheelchair basketball, all the while maintaining an academic scholarship. He had many friends and everyone treated him like the fun guy you want to hang around with.

I didn't have to make any real concessions for Barry. I'd maybe move a chair or desk so that he could get to the front of the room.

We started chatting after class. He told me about College Bowl. I told him I would tell my other classes about it to see if I could round up a few more participants.

I couldn't wait any longer; it was killing me. I had to do it.

"Do you mind if I ask you a very personal question?" I asked.

"No," he said.

"How did you get into the wheelchair? Were you in an accident?"

"I have cerebral palsy."

"CP?"

"Yes."

"Oh," I said.

What do you say? "I'm sorry"? I'm not sorry, not in that way. I don't pity Barry. I didn't know how I felt. I did feel compelled to say something more; the silence was becoming unbearable.

"You are always so happy. You have such a great disposition.

You are such an inspiration; I feel I have nothing to complain about. You handle it so well. You must have great parents," I babbled.

As it turns out, he does have a wonderful mother who told him that there was nothing he couldn't do and forced him to be self-sufficient. His father, on the other hand, wasn't nearly as supportive. And he had a ten-year-old sister who liked SpongeBob Squarepants as much as I do.

After each class meeting I learned a little more.

He did not get enough oxygen at birth, which caused the CP. The local television stations run tons of commercials from so-called lawyers asking CP victims to come forward to file lawsuits. If money was out there to be had, Barry had every right to get him some.

"Did you ever think about suing the doctor?" I asked.

"Not really. Not quite sure whose fault it was," he said.

This class was prone to going off on tangents, so I don't know how we got on this subject, but one day they started asking Barry about questions about his CP. Was he paralyzed? Could he walk? We found out that Barry can move his legs, and his mobility would improve greatly with exercise.

As a gym queen . . . I mean princess . . . I felt it was my duty to remind him to exercise every chance I got.

"Did you exercise?" I'd ask.

He'd smile sheepishly and say, "No."

"Why not?"

"Too busy."

Then he'd speed off before I could say another word. And that's how it went.

When I watch my church in a box full of its faith-healing invocations, I think of Barry. I have never seen anyone healed of a really debilitating disorder like CP. Is the problem too difficult, too complex for God? Or does He have a much higher plan for such individuals, unknown to the mind's eye? Perhaps it's that they are supposed to teach the able-bodied how to live, their disability being their gift to give.

I wonder if Barry would want to be "cured," to take up his pallet and walk. How different would his life be or have been? I have learned from Barry that the only limits are the ones we impose on ourselves. My boy didn't take lemons and make lemonade but lemon frappe, lemon meringue pie, and my personal favorite, lemon pound cake.

I only had one taker for College Bowl, and he was a no-show at the meetings. Oh, well. I wanted to know about the game, be on the inside, but I was a little embarrassed to ask to observe. When Barry invited me to a College Bowl practice, my heart leapt with joy.

"I'll be there," I said emphatically.

I didn't show up. The date and time must have slipped out of the crack in my mind. The same crack, out of which oozes information like the location of my keys or to whom I told that juicy piece of gossip. As a result, most of my conversations begin with "I'm not sure if I told you_____." And nine times out of ten, they answer, "No, you didn't tell me . . ." leaving me to wonder whom have I been talking to all this time and, whoever it is, whether they know way too much information.

Barry cornered me the next class.

"You, didn't come."

I felt smaller than "this big." I had let him down. I've flaked on other people in the past and had given some lame excuse, like, "I didn't know" or "I forgot." But this time, I really did forget. It would be pointless to explain about the crack in my mind where important and not-so-important memories seem to slip through.

"I'm sorry. Next time. I'll go. I swear."

What did I go and do that for? Swear. If I forget this time, I am going straight to hell.

"I'm bad, the worst," I said and slapped my own hand. Ow, that hurt.

He informed me of the next date. Saturday, 8 a.m. Ouch, that hurt.

So, Saturday came. I was excited. I was going to get to see smart people in action and was certain that I would know most of the answers.

I wasn't excited enough to leap out of bed on a Saturday morning. Six a.m. came. It went; then 6:15 a.m. came; and went; 6:30 a.m., too. And it, too, went; finally, 6:45. I bolted out of bed. Washed the face. Brushed the teeth. Threw on sweats and headed to the gym to get in a good thirty-five minutes of sweating and grunting.

Got it done and headed to school. The faculty coordinator, a history professor, sat on a stone bench outside waiting for the visiting team and her crew to arrive.

I approached. "I'm here for the College Bowl?"

"Are you a student?"

Oh, it was going to be good day.

Smiling from ear to ear, "Thank you," I said, "I teach here. Barry invited me."

"It's not too hard to be taken as a student here," she said dryly. Pop went my bubble.

The others arrived, including students from the HBC who came by the van load. Barry rolled up late, of course. So much for the elevator excuse.

I took the elevator up to the third floor with Barry. Yes, I could I have walked, but I wanted to keep him company. Okay, I wanted to reserve what little energy I had left. He was tickled by my appearance. Oh, so casual. No long, short, skirt with suit jackets or that infernal wig — more about her much later, much, much later. No, the answer to the question is not chemo; it's stupido. The truth is I am lazier than a slug with a thyroid problem.

The conference room had a long table and blackboards on each side. There was the clock, the buzzers, and the flashing lights to indicate who buzzed in first.

They were pleasant kids, the other folks. Didn't look like nerds, just your cool quasi hip hoppers. People from the other team were going to take turns keeping score — putting points on the board for all to see our march towards success or failure. Maybe we have a chance, I thought.

I sat in the corner taking the fly-on-the-wall approach. On our team, Barry was joined by a long-haired musician-cum-science major, a history major, and the faculty coordinator. The other team's faculty coordinator operated the clock and read the questions.

She asked the first question. What? As I was trying to process the first three words of the sentence, the buzzer rang. It was the other team. They answered correctly. It went on like this.

To me it was all a big blur of names, dates, and foreign countries. Maybe I needed carbs. Perhaps it was too early. The questions seemed overly long and complicated. And yes, I am whining. When I played "Jeopardy" at home, it seemed to go so much better. I'd lounge about watching the big screen television, casually popping off one right answer after another, albeit a hair too slow, and Alex and I seemed to say the answer at the same time, okay, I gave him a bit of a head start.

"Who is Atil . . . ?" Alex would say.

". . . Atilla the Hun. Yes! I knew it."

I'm smart. At least that is what they always told me.

The game.

The other team was whipping our ass handily. Two hundred plus points to sixty. We couldn't even break one hundred.

Despite my brain lapse, I wanted in on the game. I knew if I could get that buzzer in my hand, I could really turn it around for the team.

I wasn't called in to play. We lost. The other team didn't gloat. They were gracious winners, and we were gracious losers. There would be a next time. They invited us to come to their house to play.

Good deal. I'll be there.

I got the word from Diane, who also helped with College

Bowl, about the next meeting. Eight o'clock again. Saturday. Did the gym thing and rushed over to their place.

It was a nice campus. Not beautiful. An uneasy mixture of old and not so new. My mother attended the school when it was a teacher's college, as did my aunt, as did some of those previously mentioned cousins.

I was ready this time. Ready to play. The room was easy to find with its peeling paint, musty smell, and old windows desperately in need of repair.

There was one good thing. They had food. And plenty of it. Donuts, the greasy, sugary kind. Orange juice, individual size without the pulp. Muffins. No blood sugar problems this time. I grabbed a donut, a chocolate-covered creation from Krispy Kreme and some OJ. And I took my place in the hard desk behind my teammates. Barry, Diane, and the faculty coordinator were there, as were the rest of team.

The games began. We were getting our asses whipped, but not too badly. It seems the winds of change were blowing our way. And I actually knew some of the answers to the questions.

Diane was in the game and answering a few. She's a writer who knows a lot about literature. Barry got a few right, as did other members of the team.

Game one. We lost. Game Two. We lost. Break time. Ate some food. Diane asked me if I wanted in. It was my chance to prove myself.

I said to myself, "Yes, I can. Yes, I can."

I got in the game. I took my seat, buzzer in hand. First question. They buzzed first. Answer: Toni Morrison. I knew it but the brain and buzzer coordination was off.

Another question. Just didn't know the answer to that one. I looked at Barry who was seated next to me.

"I knew that one," I said.

He shushed me. God, I thought he was my friend.

The next question. I buzzed in. Got that one right. Answered the bonus question correctly, too. We were beginning to score some points, and they were feeling the heat. They won the game anyway.

Diane tagged in and played a round. We lost again.

Final game. Diane signaled for me to get in the game. It was close. I had my rhythm now, giving one right answer after the other. Oh yeah, there was going to be an ass whipping served up Harlem style.

We were actually leading, and I was scoring. It was now ninety to eighty-five.

We were down to the final minutes, the final questions.

"Who was the noted historian recently accused of plagiarism?" the moderator asked.

I rang in. I looked at the timer and the moderator. They nodded for me to answer.

"Stephen Foster," I said.

The moment the name left my lips, I knew it was wrong. Not Stephen Foster, Stephen Ambrose. Damn. Barry hit his hand against his head. Everyone let out a heavy, exasperated sigh. Another toss-up question was read. The other team buzzed in first and got not only that question correct but the bonus question as well, making them the winners once again.

As fate and a time mix-up would have it, that game would be my last as a College Bowler.

And dear Barry. He never let me live it down. Every time Barry saw me, he laughed and said, "Steven Foster."

But he assured me that was the closest they had ever come to scoring one hundred points. Sometimes he would tell me of a time when he, too, made a mistake. Then of course, he would laugh and say to himself, "Stephen Foster."

Humility, thy name is Carla.

smile like
you mean it

The Root of It All:
A Hair Above the Rest

She looked at me and paused.

"You don't look like yourself," she said as we walked down the stairs and out of the building.

I was meeting my friend Lila for lunch one day at her state job in a bland rectangular building on a corner in downtown Montgomery. We were on our way to grab a bite to eat — a bite was all that I could have eaten that day since I was recovering from the stomach flu.

I know. Too much information.

Lila is a special person. I really mean that. She is from Rome and has a glorious melodious accent. Every vowel is wonderfully elongated. She makes saying, "Hello" sound . . . well . . . truly fabulous.

We met in the world of books at Barnes and Noble where she also works.

She also works in the world of municipal government and just took a hiatus from her work in the world of theater. She has so many jobs, she would put a Jamaican to shame.

No one can accuse Lila of not being straightforward. So when she made that comment, I immediately took it to heart. I knew what she was talking about. She had only seen me at my most casual best — bandanna tied around my head like a kerchief, sweat pants and sweatshirts, sneakers or sandals. Here I was, wearing a long skirt, well past my ankles, a nice maroon sweater zipped up the front with a high collar, and a WIG.

Yes, it was a reddish brown mop of a thing that I had tried hopelessly to style into something resembling modern but a long way from "hip."

I hated that wig and it knew it. Never, never did it look quite right. And adding insult to injury, it made me look OLDER.

But that wig was a part of my formal, public persona. I wore it during openings for the cultural institution and even in the classroom. But as soon as those occasions were over and I went home and stepped across the threshold, I snatched that thing off and flung it on the nearest piece of furniture.

Feeling sorry for the ugly thing, I always went to retrieve it and placed it on the white Styrofoam head on my dresser. It's so weird having a disembodied head on one's dresser with no eyes to see, no ears to hear, and no mouth to protest. Note to self: Idea for a horror flick — attack of the killer wigs with their stands as accomplices.

When I came to town, I was completely natural. Hair braided. Not some expensive fancy braids that took several hours. No, I did it myself thank you. One minor problem: I don't have the gift for doing hair. Some people are just born with a bottle of gel in one hand and a styling comb in the other. My braids always turned out twisted and uneven no matter how hard I tried. And I can't make a straight part to save my life.

Those braids weren't pretty, but they were me.

But I was in Alabama, and I knew that this conservative's hairstyle was far too radical.

So, I decided to get my hair straightened. I felt I had to strike a compromise — yes, I would straighten my hair but not with chemicals. It would be with that dreaded hot comb.

Oh, the hot comb and I go way back. To the days when I used to sit between my mother's legs on that red wooden stool in our Harlem kitchen. I'd watch that hot comb with the thin metal gold teeth and wooden handle heat up on the gas stove, the smell of burning hair and grease filling my nostrils. My mother struggled as she parted my thick, coarse black hair into manageable sections and applied grease — some castor oily, foul-smelling thick stuff — to each area.

When the comb achieved the right temperature — she'd checked it by tapping her fingers gingerly and rapidly against the teeth's edge — she'd then comb though my hair with a hard tug from the root to the very end. I could feel the heat against my scalp.

It was not a gentle process, for my hair did not straighten willingly. A lot of hard comb-throughs with the instrument of torture left my hair the desired texture — bone straight and stringy.

My head was sore for days afterward. By the time I recovered, the process was set to begin again.

They say when you mess with fire there is a good chance you will get burned. And I did, many times. The comb nicked my temple, ears, and the nape of my neck, leaving burns and scabs all over my little head.

My mother didn't start straightening my hair until after a trip "home" to Montgomery when, at the suggestion of some idle-brained relative, who looked at my thick locks and found them distasteful, did she begin to apply the torturous process on young me.

So here I was, at the place where it all began. I was getting my hair pressed, the formal name for the hot comb treatment. Damn the circle of life.

I was never satisfied. It was too straight. And like in days past, it hurt like hell. My once-thick, healthy hair began to thin — falling out from the root, breaking from the ends.

I tried one hair dresser after another. Each one looked at my hair and agreed to do it.

"No problem," they'd say.

That was until the hairdressers washed it and it went back to its natural, happier, nappier state. Although I had lost quite a few strands, my hair was still very thick. The once quoted price of twenty-five dollars was always doubled when all was said and done. The reason, "I didn't know you had so much hair."

The money thing was only the half of it. It was the caustic backhanded insults and the lack of love for us nappy-headed sisters that really got to me.

While sitting in yet another salon, I heard a beautician refer to unpressed, unprocessed, unaltered hair as "off-the-boat hair."

Sometimes I can be quite the literalist and metaphors seem to elude me, but I got that one. Oh boy and how. The boat to which she was referring was a slave ship.

Too angry to protest. Too scared to, too. Would you open your trap if someone were standing over you, blazing hot comb in hand with the ability to render you completely bald or worse? No, the risk was far too great. So I kept my mouth shut, knowing that she was referring to the likes of me with my Africanesque locks.

And there I was getting my hair straightened to conform to a society that has yet to embrace the concept of being black and proud.

Needless to say, I did not return.

Always willing to give it just one more try, I decided to go to yet another salon. The place came highly recommended from a friend of one of my students.

Why not? I thought. Maybe this time it will be better. That's me, forever the optimist.

So, I went to the other side of town, traveled the wrong way down a one-way street, and navigated my car around potholes that could swallow the biggest supertanker SUV. Finally, I found it. It turned out to be a powder-blue cinder-block house resembling some odd fairy tale castle. Oh yeah, it was a fairy tale all right, complete with a gruff woman and her able-bodied assistant ready to sock it to poor, innocent me. The owner and head beautician was a short, large-breasted older woman with a mocha complexion and Sharon Osborne hair, who was always scurrying to and fro.

The salon was located downstairs. Upstairs was her residence to which she often retreated in the middle of some process only to return much later after one or all of my body parts had fallen asleep or after my neck had developed permanent shampoo-bowl marks.

I often wondered exactly what she was doing up there.

Her assistant, a darker, taller woman with a processed curl, said very little but occasionally smiled sheepishly for no apparent reason.

Like all of the others, the hairdresser, whom I will call Miss M., was happy to see me . . . at first. Then she started doing my hair and became increasingly annoyed with my naturally thick, coarse mane.

One day while at the shampoo bowl, Miss M. leaning over me, her fingers briskly rubbing my scalp and lathering my locks, her breasts hitting me about the face, nearly putting my eye out, said the unthinkable.

"Have you thought about getting a (chemical) relaxer? It would really help."

Oh, hell no. She's gone too far now.

How could she suggest such a thing? I thought.

But I said, "No. No thank you, I'm not interested."

She then looked at me askance and asked, "Why?"

"I just don't want chemicals in my hair," I said, trying to be firm but not rude.

The way she looked at me the first time I said this, you'd have thought I had said that I eat small children but I like to salt and pepper them first.

A determined not-so-little something, she'd ask the same question every time I visited, thinking perhaps she could either wear me down or cause me to slip up.

And every time, she treated my polite declines as if they were the protests of a willful child.

After awhile, she tried another approach. She complained that pressing my hair with a straightening comb was causing her great physical pain. When relating her oft-told tale, she would grab her arm and wince. Her behavior was more drama queen than dire; and she was both dismayed and surprised that I wasn't moved by her performance.

Those anxious and seemingly endless hours at the salon was the cost associated with turning my very kinky hair into medium-length locks of straight, moveable hair. You know, the kind you can run your fingers though without them getting caught in some tangled mess. The kind that allows you to take a shower without the cap. The kind they call, "good hair." The kind my fair-skinned, hazel-eyed cousins have.

If you haven't figured it out by now, I don't have "good hair" but what they call "bad hair." We bad hair people are supposed to fear water, in all of its forms. This relatively simple organic compound can reduce once-confident women to sniveling, weeping masses of flesh and cause the most luxurious mane to resemble something akin to a Bride of Frankenstein hairdo.

Don't get me wrong. Just because I had my hair pressed doesn't mean that I didn't love my hair. I loved my hair then, and I love my hair now. Jet black and coarse. Strong and invincible, with the ability to withstand the harshest of chemicals and the hottest of hot combs. And flexible. I've worn many different styles, including the "I think I want dreadlocks but I am afraid of the commitment" unruly braided hair look.

My absolute favorite was the shaved very short natural, a style which I wore for many years. There was nothing like running my fingers along, (note not through), my freshly sheared head and feeling the gentle prickles of each strand.

Oh, freedom. Finally, wash-and-wear hair. No need to fear water anymore.

I didn't come to this hairstyle easily. I got my first haircut at eighteen, and it was only a trim. I was led to believe by others that if you cut off your hair, it won't grow back.

Well, I was away at school when I did the unthinkable. I went to some fashionable salon in downtown Chicago and had them take a little of the ends and shape up my hair. For the first time in my life, I actually had a hairstyle. Well, hell, I went crazy after that cutting it off into some shaggy do. And it grew back every time. Take that, you old wives' tale.

Never one to leave well enough alone, I decided to take it to the next level. But this time it was going to be different, more extreme. Not only short, but natural. Practically bald. What would my head look like? Would it be some lumpy, bumpy mess? Would it look like it should be thrown down a football field in a forward pass? Would I have the face for short, short, short hair?

It wasn't as if I was going to miss my hair. I had had it with hair. Totally overrated. And mine at the time was a mess, an absolute mess. Broken, uneven strands. Ends split nearly up the shaft. So it was easy to part with, or so I thought until the hairdresser took a whack at a chunk of my hair and kept on whacking. It was not looking too good at first. But when you make decision like that, you can't go back. She kept cutting and cutting. I started looking better, then began to look great.

And my head turned out to be round and smooth. And I was loving it. Those were the days . . . .

Back to 'Bama.

I had it up to here with Le Drama Queen and her constant complaints. So, I stopped going.

I was back to where I started — doing my own hair, braiding it myself.

There was just one problem. I was still in Alabama. And those crazy braids that I loved so were the problem in the first place.

Solution. Wear a wig. Why? I guess it was the "when in Rome thing . . ." Good hair yes, but without the hairdresser drama.

One day, running late, I barreled into her, Miss Wiggs', room. We had separate rooms; it was better that way. I would have found it disconcerting to awake in the middle of the night to find her "staring" at me.

I stopped abruptly in front of the dresser. I looked at her resting lopsided on the head. I knew that she knew . . . about my fear . . . not of the dreaded H_2O or even the hot comb, but the fear of standing out, of being different for yet another reason.

I poked at the Styrofoam head's "eyes" and pinched its nose. It didn't cry out, and neither did she. Completely harmless. Then I yanked the wig off the head and positioned it at the toe of my foot.

I kicked that hairy thing out of my life and told it to take that disembodied head with it.

No, I was going to wear my own hair thank you — underneath a wrap. I got the idea from one of my students who, after class, showed me how it was done. I'm no India Arie and clearly no Erika Badu, but I must admit that the style was the most "me" that I had been in a very long time.

When I wore one of my colorful wraps to work at the university, a colleague commented that I looked, "very ethnic" that day.

I love her dearly, but I wanted to say, "Darling, I look ethnic everyday."

Face Value

My mother always told me that she wanted me to possess the Three B's — to be Black, Beautiful, and Brilliant.

Perhaps, it was a seventies thing that started and ended with activist Angela Davis. According to my mother, Angela had them — the three Bs — but unfortunately, she made a very radical left turn. As I was washing dishes, mopping the floor, or performing some other kind of housekeeping chore, my mother would tell me the necessity of possessing these three important attributes.

From time to time, she had told me that I was smart. And I am, of course, undeniably black — but beautiful? That's another story entirely.

In keeping with her Southern heritage, there was nothing said really, at least not directly. She, sighing as she combed my thick hair, eyed me up and down just before I left the house, and stated as she fixed a collar, brushed off a sometimes invisible piece of lint, "I have to make you over."

There was no real makeover per se, just the addition of some earrings or lip gloss, which she insisted improved my appearance greatly.

A mother's work was never done.

My shoulders were too broad.

"Don't sit like that," she'd say as I pressed my hands down on the sofa, bed, or chair trying to make my back straight. "You're going to make your shoulders broad."

And my lips were too full.

"Do this," my mother said as she sucked in her lips making her look like she needed a good pair of dentures.

I'd imitate her in an effort to make my relatively thin lips look even thinner.

And my nose was too broad.

She'd apply a careful pinch to my proboscis every now and then; and, for my part, I'd try not to smile or look any way that might make my nose broader.

All this was a part of the makeover process.

I learned to never fully trust a compliment or even my own reflection in the mirror. When I think I look okay, I inevitably find something that needs to be fixed, a flaw that I have missed.

"I did not see that scar yesterday. Is that a mole? Are those lines underneath my eyes?"

I'd begun to fret, add extra moisturizer, do some facial exercises or take an extra vitamin.

My mother once told me, "I'm your mother; would I lie to you?" No, but perhaps someone has lied to her.

I told a therapist once about my mother and her quest to make me over. She looked at me askance not quite getting what I was saying.

Several years, a few therapists, and scores of self-help books later, I have come to terms with my imperfect looks. So, I am a combination of good parts, nice teeth, sometimes nice hair, not-so-bad skin, decent legs, and a great smile, the sum of these parts making a relatively attractive whole.

I wondered what it would be like to have a mother who looked into my eyes and saw "pretty." "Beautiful" would be asking too much.

Perhaps I supported the cultural institution's new receptionist's efforts to make her daughter into a kiddie beauty pageant princess because it was nice to see a mother who thought her child was "beautiful."

Being a receptionist is no walk in the park. I had financed part of my grad school in L.A. answering call after call at high-end post production houses — being very close to the action but never really a part of it — always having to be "on" with a bright smile and a pleasant voice.

So, I always had a soft spot in my heart for the receptionist — telephone stuck to the ear, ass stuck to the chair.

We (the corporate "we"), at the cultural institution, had just gotten rid of the last one, a big brown-skinned mama, with sculpted orange-blond hair. The one who thought all black people drank wine coolers and not wine. Sista had a habit of wearing too much perfume and spending too much time eating at her desk, which was always a mess. The worse of it was her bionic hearing. We were in very close quarters, literally inches from one another, separated by the felt and metal of gray cubicle walls. You could hold a conversation with the person in the next cubicle without leaving your seat. If someone was on the phone, there was an unwritten rule: If you hear every word of a conversation and it has nothing to do with you, ignore it.

Perhaps Girlfriend didn't get the memo; I really don't know what her problem was, but she would ask you about your telephone conversations and acted as if it was her right to do so. No matter how softly you whispered, she heard and commented on every word.

I wanted to ask, "Does none of your business mean anything to you?"

Her replacement was a pretty, big boned, strawberry blond with clear skin and a slightly foggy, brain whose feet dragged across the carpet when she walked. Pleasant enough but no real personality. She was promoted for her lack of effort.

The revolving door swung around again, and we got a new girl, a petite young woman with long brown hair and pale, slightly freckled skin, who looked no older than sixteen but was in her mid-twenties. She had an edge to her like someone who had been through some stuff. She wasn't rough or unpleasant, just professional.

I was always bored. And when I was bored, I talked to whomever would listen. I liked going around the office and visiting my fellow workers spreading a bit of cheer. I worked in public relations and felt it was my duty to apply those same principles to the workplace. The director, a dour man, did not share my philosophy.

Cathy, the new girl, was pleasant and chatty. I was happy to have someone close by to talk to.

On her first day, I offered my services — bathroom, smoke, and lunch breaks if needed. And I would answer the phone if I found it ringing too long because she was giving someone directions from Alaska.

We chatted about stuff. She did a lot of the talking. I did a lot of the listening. Cathy was a single mother with two preschool-age girls. She earned not much more than I did when I graduated from college many years ago. Even then, I couldn't imagine trying to raise two children such a salary. She was a teen mom and her mom had been one as well. She lived with her father's parents, who did their best. Cathy was an honors student and had attended college briefly. She loved her children and had no regrets. Cathy was good mom, always ordering books and flash cards for the kids.

One day Cathy came in, her face aglow, a couple of small packets in her hand.

"I have some pictures of my daughter's beauty pageant," she said, all smiles.

When she told me that her daughter had entered a beauty pageant, I didn't know what to think.

"Sure, I'll take a look at them," I said.

What I saw were pictures of a petite little girl with blond curls dressed in a party dress, white patent leather shoes, and a smile from ear to ear. There was another of her at the beauty salon, mother by her side, the girl's blond locks twisted around big pink rollers.

She proudly told me that her daughter had won a fifty dollar savings bond.

"Pretty good for her first pageant," she smiled.

I smiled as visions of Jon Benet Ramsey . . . and Donna, the girl from my first two years in college, swirled in my head.

They called Donna the Ivory Snow Girl because she had a flawless complexion, the color of slightly singed milk. She always has a pleasant smile, which was in direct contrast to my then perpetual scowl.

Donna was always all smiles as she tilted her head slightly, letting her soft brown, medium-length hair frame her face. It would be of no surprise to you that Donna, of course, had good hair.

And she was smart . . . not a genius, but she was willing to work hard for her B+ average. She was the apple of every boy's eye, but her heart belonged to one and one only.

I became chummy with Donna after my former friends joined a sorority. She lived down the hall from me. After I tired of receiving poor grades, I decided to go to class and do a little studying. Donna and I weren't the best of friends; we had so little in common. I had the feeling she was just trying to be her usual polite self — nodding on cue, smiling on cue, giving the uh-huhs when appropriate. It didn't matter; I was so lonely and desperate, I would have spoken to a brick wall.

The following year, we ended up in the same dorm again. It was located in the middle of the sorority quad, a fine early twentieth-century three-story stone and brick house that was more like a townhouse than a dorm, with its hardwood floors and large bay windows.

Donna and I served as elected officials of the residence, social co-chairpersons — a very strange position for an anti-social person like myself. We organized such quaint gatherings as a Valentine's Day party. As a part of our official duties, Donna and I had to attend dorm meetings with the officers.

The Ivory Snow girl did her best not to ruffle any feathers, perhaps already having set her sights on a bigger office . . . Homecoming Queen.

I saw it in the paper a year after Donna left the dorm, her picture with the words Homecoming Queen written across the top. Although I never attended any of the homecoming festivities, I always seemed to stumble upon the parade. The goings-on were mainly for alums — to soften them up, get them all misty-eyed and nostalgic. It was all part of an innocuous master plan. The alumni would begin to believe that the college experience was a lot better than they remembered. So when they received the numerous requests for money via mail, they would send sentimental, tear-stained checks with a couple of numbers followed by multiple zeros.

Running for Homecoming Queen requires a vote by your peers. Since I never considered myself anyone's peer, feeling a cut below the rest, old girl did not receive my vote. No, I don't hate her. And I'm not . . . wasn't jealous either. She had the hair, the skin, the boyfriend, what did she need with another crown? There should be a limit on such things — two per person, and by no means, no more than three.

Even without my vote, she won. I stood on the main street watching her pass by on her float, waving like royalty, her handsome chocolate-brown king by her side. She was the first, or one of the first, black Homecoming Queens, the pinnacle of crossover success.

I saw Donna, years later, in the Atlanta airport as I was trying to navigate my way through the maze of moving stairs and underground railways en route to my connecting flight. She looked essentially the same. The Ivory Snow complexion had dulled a bit and there was a weariness on her face. Her hairstyle, current back then, now looked a bit outdated. She was working as a sales rep for a computer company. Her boyfriend was gone and there was no mention of a husband. We said our Hi's and How are you doing?s and went our separate ways. Time is a sweet avenger.

Enough about her. (How many times do I have to tell you, I'm not jealous? Not anymore.)

Cathy's confidence in her daughter's winning ability may have rested in what was on her daughter's head and not in it. My darling, she is a blond for God's sake. Blond is big in Alabama — deemed truly superior and all-powerful. To have a tow-headed child is truly a gift from God. The world becomes your oyster.

Sure, blond is an interesting hair color. Nice, but not better in any way. In my humble opinion, dark-haired women seem to have deeper, more sensuous beauty than their lighter-haired counterparts. I thought we, as a nation, were long over the blond obsession, having merely reduced it to some fashion statement.

But not in 'Bama.

I learned the real deal during one of the institution's in-house mailings. It was someone's bright idea that if we did the mailings ourselves and did not farm them out to a more efficient company, we would save money. So we spent hours stuffing envelopes, sealing them and our fingers with glue sticks, and sorting them by zip code.

This nice, mindless task diverted our attention from other mindless tasks and gave us much-needed sanctioned chatting time. It was there where I learned about the blond, among other things. I don't know how we got on the subject. One of my co-workers was pregnant, a bottled blond who was pondering the hair color of her future offspring. A pretty raven-haired girl with olive skin and buoyant personality said she hoped the child would be born blond. Other young women in the room, all white, nodded in agreement. Blond was not just good but highly desirable.

Cathy had two children, but only one of them was a blond. After she settled in awhile, she had pictures of them on her desk. One was the pixie blond; the other was obviously mixed race with skin the color of cinnamon, a head full of long, thick, curly, jet-black hair, a broad nose, and a big smile.

Both were equally adorable.

I asked the questions, that perhaps I should not have asked.

"Do they have any trouble? Are they close?" "Any trouble" was defined as enduring racist remarks, snide asides, or awkward stares.

She said, "They are as close as any sisters could be — each one very protective of the other." At the pageant, the cinnamon one yelled out, "That's my sister." I sighed with relief but still was thinking that, in the future, people with a penchant for dividing and conquering and categorizing will cause sister to turn on sister.

I did a story on diversity for a local parenting magazine about talking to your kids about race and ethnicity. According to the experts, children see color but not race. They don't affix things like personality characteristics, good or bad, to skin color. It's not uncommon for a child to refer to her black friends as brown for, to them, brown is just a description, not a condemnation, or an assessment. But as children age, the schoolyard comes to resemble more of a battleground, one in which race can become a weapon or a target.

People, visitors, volunteers, and fellow employees, often passed by Cathy's desk and asked to see pictures of the children. They would have a smile on their face when they picked up the flower-shaped frame. But the moment they laid eyes on the children in its photo, one pink and blond, the other light brown and brunette, their smiles became strained as they nervously placed the picture down — sometimes saying nothing and other times just giving a polite word, "nice."

As much as I admired Cathy, it did trouble me that most of her earnings were going to pay for pageant items — fees, a new outfit, shoes, etc. She and her friends entered their children into competition. All they spoke of were dresses, judges, and walking and talking the pageant way.

She learned how to sew and made a cute red sequined outfit for one of the events.

Her daughter was a natural, or so Cathy said, and wanted

to do it. Cathy did coach her but just a little bit — practicing the walk, reviewing possible questions and answers.

She often became stressed out about the details. How should she walk? What are the judges looking for? Where can I find a dress?

I hate to see anyone in pain. So I did what I probably shouldn't have done — offered to help. She had an assignment for me. Look online and find a dress. I had a computer at home and she didn't. So there I was, early in the morning, sleep still in my eyes and around my mouth, surfing the Internet for pageant dresses.

My next assignment was to find this obscure tape of a children's song which would be perfect for the talent portion of the completion.

Her daughter continued to win. No money, but she did get to ride on a float during a parade. Just like Donna.

With each pageant came more expenses. The big one was coming up. She showed me the flyer; it had the word "international" in the title. For this one, she had to actively solicit funds. She asked for my help in creating ad copy and a list of places that might be interested in purchasing ads for inclusion in a commemorative book.

I helped. I gave her ten dollars for an ad. All the while, I was thinking that Cathy's effort and money could be spent on better things, like finding a better-paying job. She tried to look for a better-paying job, although half-heartedly, all of her efforts being focused on the big day: the qualifying pageant for the international competition.

I felt protective of her like a big sister or a little mama. They, the corporate "they," were always riding her about reading the newspaper or doing something else at her desk. I couldn't figure out why and neither could she. She never let anything interfere with her work. She did a great job and was always trying to devise more efficient ways of doing things. But all "they" wanted her to do was sit and wait for the phone to ring.

To keep her company, I'd sit at one of the guest chairs

and chat. Well, as luck would have it, the powers that be weren't fond of our chats. Her supervisor approached us one afternoon, hands on her hips. She said a few words to Cathy. I said something. The supervisor said something. It developed into a mess, with the supervisor all but threatening to give me a schoolyard whipping. Although, we were both out of line, I was the one asked to apologize.

Well, you know that didn't happen.

But, I regret that I might have made things even worse for Cathy, who was really under lock and key after the incident.

I knew my days were numbered and began making plans. A short time later, I walked out of the door with a lot of memories and no regrets.

Well before pageant day, I received some information in the mail about the festivities from Cathy. I was planning to go. Cathy promised to call me before the big day to give me more details.

The call never came.

I did receive a call from some quickie loan place about serving as a reference for her. I said no. It would not have fixed the problem, whatever it might have been, and just would have made it worse. And anyway, I was angry, the least she could have done was to have contacted me, let me know what was happening, asked my permission.

But enough about me.

Cathy knew that the clock was about the strike midnight, but she continued to do nothing. It was all about the pageant.

She was eventually let go. I heard she was working at some restaurant on the bypass. I was going to call her at her job. Maybe see her on her lunch break.

That never happened.

I'm not sure if her daughter won. It doesn't matter really. Winning wouldn't have changed much. It wouldn't have made the slope any less steep.

Maybe after it's all done, she will have a closet full of pageant dresses, a crown, sashes, and remembrances of brighter days of hope and promise of what could have been and never was.

The high stakes game of beauty and fame. It's the poor woman's version of the three-picture deal, the record contract, the sports deal with the signing bonus and multimillion dollar shoe endorsement. Many come to play, but so very few win.

Rather recently, I've noticed people commenting that my mother and I look alike — more like sisters than mother and daughter, which may be great for her but not for me. No, I was never my mother's idea of beautiful although she no longer tries to make me over; at least not overtly. She has come to realize that my shoulders won't narrow and my lips are not getting any smaller.

I'm not sure why. Is it because she is more comfortable with me or with herself?

_____

Like Fine Wine

One fine day, as I was cruising down the bypass, I caught my reflection in the rearview mirror. Okay one doesn't catch one's reflection; it takes a deliberate effort to look into the mirror. I can't pass by a pane of glass without checking out my reflection. It's not because of narcissism but necessity, for I always miss something, like toothpaste on the corner of my mouth or a piece of hair that has gone astray. (Where is Mom when I really need a "makeover"?)

So, I was cruising along, trying to stay in my lane when I spot what I think to be a GRAY HAIR. Still cruising and now cursing, I tried to take a closer look as the car weaves in and out of the lane. Someone honks the horn, and I get a hold of myself. Red light. I practically pressed my face against the rearview mirror. It *was* a gray hair. I yanked and yanked, and ouch, it was out. And I was nearly passed out from the pain and exhaustion.

I'm not ready to have a gray hair. I was and am but a mere girl.

Don't laugh. Who cares if I can count my age in dog years?

I know that the momentous occasion of my becoming a grown-up, would dare not pass me by. I feel that I am getting close, but I am still not quite there.

Is becoming a woman merely physical? Do the fine lines that mark a face define it? Or do creaky joints? I have had creaky bones since I was a child. Clearly, I was no more a woman then than I am now.

When is the onset of womanhood? Does menstruation mark its beginnings? Just because one is capable of bearing a child doesn't mean that one becomes a woman. Girls as young as nine- or ten-years-old can menstruate. Perhaps, in another century when people bore children at a much younger age, menstruation marked the beginning of womanhood, but this definition has no relevance in today's society.

I have come to conclude that womanhood is a gradual process that perhaps is primarily a state of mind rather than an external transformation. You evolve. It happens to different people at different stages which can be labeled as "pre-woman," "almost there," and "Yeah, what do you want to know?" Sometimes the evolution never takes place. Never? Think of the childish adults you know.

And although not clearly defined, the manifestation of womanhood is clearly recognizable. In other words, you know a real woman when you see her.

Womanhood. Its development comes from the realization that some things are just beyond one's control. Life is too short and you, for all of your wisdom, really don't know very much at all. Real women have inner strength which is not to be underrated.

And you won't find this strength at your local gym. Pump iron until you rip your shirt. Kickbox until your thighs become rock hard, and you still won't get any closer to becoming a woman.

I have consulted women (of the real sort) who have told me that once I get older I will have the right to do and say what I want. I can't wait. I've been speaking my mind for years so that when I become a woman, I will be ready.

I adore these great ladies, or broads, whose behavior is marked by an ease and a knowing that there is no one to please but themselves.

I love old people. Sassy things. Spry. Like Lila B. (who just happens to have the same name as that other feisty woman), a W.W. II Pearl Harbor nurse who authored her memoirs at age eighty-eight. We also met at the bookstore.

I hung out in the bookstore. It was the preferred meeting place for a disparate group of intellectuals, bibliophiles, military types from the war college, moms who needed to get out of the house, and those just trying to get a free read.

The bookstore was where I caught my breath, pondered my dream. Time slowed as I read magazines on the benches by the racks or sat in the overstuffed chairs, springs and padding worn out by hours of contemplation by a variety of patrons and their variously sized butts.

It was my refuge where I came to get away from the sadness and quiet desperation and from the beige walls and the stale, recycled air. A series of left turns got me there, which was wonderful for a directionally challenged person like me.

Lila B. She attended my writers' workshop a few years ago. It really wasn't mine, per se. I only gave my presentation, my two cents.

Lila, the other one, the Italian who works like a Jamaican, called asking me to conduct a writers' workshop. My partner was going to be an English professor from the university. A mild panic started to set in.

What did I know about writing? I had just starting to write some very opinionated op-eds and fluffy-headed feature articles. It wasn't until two years later when the flow of work turned into a trickle, that I actually called myself a "writer."

The tug of war began — the right brain came up with neat ideas. The left brain bought the index cards, books, and handouts and meticulously rehearsed the presentation.

You know I love an audience. You know I need an audience. I feared that few people would show up. It was football Saturday and most Alabamians were either rolling with the Tide or chasing the Tiger.

Game Day. I walked into the store, which was practically empty, and headed towards the back. Tables were placed together especially for the occasion and the chairs, now empty, were arranged in a semicircle in front of them. I sat down and arranged my papers and books on the table and practiced by looking out into the nonexistent audience.

My co-presenter, Peggy, arrived. She was a cool, collegiate writer type, with short gray hair, a neat, funky, dangly silver charm bracelet, and a white cotton shirt. I was probably wearing my wig. Wig or no wig, I am sure I was having a bad hair day.

Peggy was the cool kind of woman I wanted to be when I grew up. She was a poetess and a professor. I was an opinionated wanna-be writer.

There was a division of labor, insisted upon by my left brain. I would cover the practical side of journalism and writing for the screen, big and small; she would tackle poetry and stirring one's creative juices.

Lila B. and her friend were the first to arrive, dressed in a little less than Sunday best but still quite fashionable. Lila B. had snow-white hair. Her companion had short brown hair and oversized glasses. Both looked more worldly than grand-motherly. Don't expect milk and cookies from this pair.

They sat in the front row.

"I want to write a book," Lila B. yelled from her seat, "Are you going to tell me how to get my book published?"

I smiled. Oh how quaint, I thought. Old people are so delightful.

"No, we are going to talk about writing, articles, and poetry and stuff like that. But I am sure the store has some books on publishing; you ought to check them out," I said.

That wasn't what she wanted to hear.

"I'm a Pearl Harbor nurse and I want to write my memoirs," said Lila B.

"Yeah," said her partner.

So precious, those two, I thought.

More people began to trickle in. About fifteen. Pretty good for a football Saturday.

The two old ladies were paying attention to our every word. They even took notes.

I gave my schpiel, took questions from the audience. Peggy did her dance as well.

Afterwards, the older women took the handouts. They thanked me and went on their way.

Fast forward one year later.

I walk into the bookstore and on the display rack is a book by, who else? None other than Lila B! I'll be damned. She wrote the book and had it published, too. It's rather discomforting to have been bested by an older woman. I guess success should not be wasted on the young.

Another year passed. I was attending a book signing at the store and chatting with the author. I looked over and saw Lila B. sitting in the café reading a book. She looked great — hadn't aged a day.

I approached her. "Do you remember me?"

"No," she said.

It's because she's old I convinced myself.

"I gave the writer's workshop a couple of years ago. You were there," I said voice cracking, ego splintering.

She looked puzzled for a bit and smiled.

"Yes," she said, wanting to get back to her reading.

"It's great seeing you," I said.

"Yes," she said still smiling. How soon they forget.

I was lingering about, chatting again with the other author and getting the low-down on the publishing biz, when I couldn't help but overhear Lila B. tell someone about her travels.

"I don't go anywhere very much in my eighties," she told a friend.

Did I hear this woman correctly? I had to investigate. Call it what you will; I had to know.

Whom to ask? The other Lila.

I caught up with her by one of the stacks.

"Hey, Lila, how old is Lila B.?"

"She is ninety."

"Ninety?!"

My God, with the exception of forgetting who I was, (even I forget who I am sometimes) her mind was a steel trap. She still drives and even serves as an escort for some of her younger friends.

Lila B. gives talks at local schools about World War II. And . . . she is a consummate marketing maven who is in the middle of the second run of her autobiography. Her schedule is always full, but she does find time to read.

After the reunion, I saw Lila B. a great deal.

"I learn something new everyday," she told me once.

I asked her why she didn't write her memoirs sooner. She said, "It just didn't happen that way."

Despite the human tragedy she had witnessed, including the death of her husband due to a massive heart attack, she confessed, that, after all was said and done, she, had lived a charmed life.

My Alabama grandmother, Grandma N., lived to be eighty-two years old. She died on my birthday. Unlike Lila B., she never wanted to learn more about her world beyond the evening news.

Grandma N. didn't have much formal schooling. Never had use for it. In the world according to Grandma N., education should serve only as a means to get you a "good" job, paying "good" money, because too much learning is a dangerous thing.

She had no interest in preserving anything for posterity, including documenting her personal history in any fashion. When my sister, a gourmet cook (She's a gourmet cook, and I'm a gourmet eater.) asked my grandmother to write down recipes in a journal which she provided, my grandmother tossed it aside and said under her breath, "You write it."

Grandma N. stopped driving years before she should have and sat in a dark family room. How ironic. Few family members came to visit except for major holidays.

I never feared growing older, having been fortunate enough to have wonderful role models. My friend Jane is a fifty-year-old, fabulous, fun-loving math professor. She helped me to understand the reason why math exists. Honestly, I thought it was just to frustrate me and ruin my standardized test scores. Thanks to her, I still may not be able to add two and two, but I no longer think of math as a hostile force.

I also committed to lifting weights with her once a week. She knows form and function and can out-lift me by at least thirty pounds. Under Jane's tutelage, I may even go sleeveless one day.

Jane is just one the countless older friends I've had over the years, friends who could show me how it can be done with grace and style.

Sources of inspiration can be found closer to home as well.

My mother, a fiercely competitive gym rat who laps others young and old as she power walks around the track, intends to rewrite the paradigm making one's sixties the new thirties. I signed her up for her first health club many years ago, and she's been on a mission ever since. Mother is about business, for she intends to keep her body healthy and strong and spread the good word to everyone who will listen.

But I discovered there was another side to aging.

Shortly before she died, I went with my Grandmother N. to a local nursing home on the other side of town, to visit a deaf relative. I was nervous, fearing the worse — feeble individuals toddling around, aimless and hopeless. I never could have imagined what I saw. Men and women in wheelchairs lined the hall. A putrid, fecal-smelling odor permeated the entire place, making me gag, and disoriented Alzheimer's patients wandered the halls.

We finally made it to his room. There he laid, his body twisted, arthritis immobilizing the once self-sufficient man who studied at the state's school for the deaf. He was happy to see us I guess. We didn't know sign language, and he couldn't see well enough to read lips. We stayed awhile; my grandmother spoke gently as she helped him drink a Coke with a straw. I wanted to cry and couldn't sleep soundly for days afterward.

Many years ago when I was small and my sister even smaller, we went to visit my New York grandmother, who was in the last stages of lung cancer, at a place called Calvary, a residence for the terminally ill.

Located in the Bronx, it had lush gardens and colorful flowers and benches where patients sat with their caretakers. The sun always shone brightly through the large bay windows of the sitting room. Our last visit was a particularly poignant and frightening one. My grandmother, hair thinning, her skin taupe, asked my father to take her home.

I remember the look in his eyes. Sad and resolute.

"Mother, you can't come home," he said.

Her eyes widened. Her once-booming voice now thin and shrill as she tried to scream at the top of her lungs to her only son, her only child, whom she had controlled since birth.

"What do you mean, I'm not coming home?"

My mother quickly ushered my sister and me out of the room and into the hallway. Our small minds were barely able to comprehend what was going on.

There was more yelling, but I could make out what they were saying.

When Dad finally came to meet us, he looked worn-out and profoundly sad and said nothing on our long ride home.

I had buried that memory in one of those crevices in my brain. After the visit to the nursing home, it came oozing back.

I had begun to fear what I had always embraced.

I have sad days and not so sad ones. No different from anyone else I guess. But rather than slit my wrists with a butter knife or jump off of a curb, I choose to look at the bright side of things and vow to never let a few gray hairs and creaky bones make me forget the possibilities of my every tomorrow.

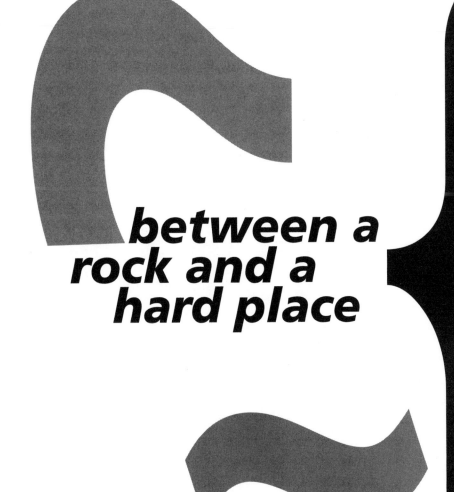

between a rock and a hard place

For the Love of God

"**N**ow I lay me down to sleep, I pray the Lord my soul to keep. And God, I'd like to thank You for the many blessings you have bestowed upon me . . . My keys . . . Thanks for shining your eternal light that enabled me to find my most precious keys under that stack of papers on my countertop. And merciful God, thank you for my brand new Mercedes, an answer to my prayers. What a blessing that car has been. There's nothing like going from zero to eighty in six seconds . . ."

It's a familiar prayer with a brand new twist for a brand new day. A bit far-fetched? Don't bet on it.

If you haven't noticed, God has had a makeover. I don't know when it happened exactly. It seemed that God went away for a while — taking a long sabbatical in the sixties and returning sometime in the eighties. Well, God is back with a whole new look, which He has sported on the covers of popular magazines. Funny, this nouveau God acts a whole lot like Santa Claus with an even greater generous streak. He wants to give you things. What things? Anything your little heart desires.

This is not your grandmother's God. Oh, no. He loves you and because He loves you, He wants to give you that big, shiny, new SUV. Why? Because you deserve it and because you are a child of God. What loving parent wouldn't want to give His precious offspring the best of everything? If you pray, it will come. Wrapped in a big ribbon. It seems like God is a guilty parent giving you the desires of your heart because He doesn't have time to spend quality time with you.

Why doesn't He have time? He's too busy looking for lost keys and shopping for SUVs. I love God just as much as the next person, but praying for a Mercedes or to find my lost keys in the morning seems a bit too petty and personal. I like my God at a distance, doing the heavy lifting, sizing up the big picture.

And this new God — the good time God — doesn't want you to deal with life's unpleasantness. No pain and suffering, thank you. We will have none of that.

Hey, who says that pain and suffering is a bad thing? Perhaps, therein lies the true blessing — to feel something deeply, even if that something is pain. Isn't the ability to feel and feel deeply what makes us truly human?

I believe in God — not the good time, candy man God. Although it would be nice if He existed because I could use some extra stuff and my absent-minded behind would definitely benefit from some help finding my keys in the morning.

I believe in God, but I have trouble with organized religion.

Organized religion (him with a small "h") and I have had an on-again and off-again relationship over the years. It seems like all we'd ever do is fight. Sometimes the disputes were over money. I'm never sure if he really loves me for me or for what I can give him in that collection plate every Sunday. At other times, we were at odds because he was not listening to my needs. There was no give and take . . . just take.

Every time we'd have a falling out, I promised myself that I wouldn't go back to him. But all he had to do was wear a shiny new suit, sing one of those sweet gospel songs, talk that smooth talk, and I was smitten all over again.

So given our history, why was I rushing to church every Wednesday and Sunday? I don't know why really. That's a lie. I do know.

When I first came to Alabama, I didn't go church regularly, but I was at the gym. Five days a week. Every week. The facility was a thoroughly modern place, sleekly designed in black and silver metal. Very high tech. It was kind of out of place architecturally in Alabama, which is known for more traditional decor. It may not have been traditional in appearance but it was traditional in demeanor.

There was strict dress code. No bare midriff. No thongs. The proper footwear must be worn at all times.

No shoes. No shirts. No service.

This gym was no meat market. Strictly for the genteel set. Yoga, please. Step aerobics thank you. No hip hop or funk aerobics. You will cycle to music that dares not be too loud.

So there I was, very much accustomed to shaking my ass in some funkefied aerobics class led by the latest sensation who went by the names of Truly or Devorah. This gym's most popular and well-attended classes were for the older, more mature set. That should tell you something right there. I wasn't too distressed by the slower pace. My ass-shaking days are quickly coming to a close anyway.

I met Tanya at the gym. I had seen her around on the treadmill and in spinning class. One day, we started talking about life. Sometimes hers. Sometimes mine. God was often weaved into the conversation as well.

Tanya was a raw-boned, brown-skinned girl with long thin braids which were swept up and kept in place with a wide metal barrette. Broad hips. Big legs. A sister who could squat two hundred pounds on a bad day, she had a swagger that would rival John Wayne's. This wife and mother of three had no job. Her husband didn't want her to work, which was fine with her — people "got on her nerves" anyway. She also had "a don't start none, won't be none" kind of attitude. Tanya was the kind of hard knock girl I remember from my

Catholic grade school days, a girl such as Melinda.

Oh dear sweet, Melinda. She was always threatening to kick my ass for some unknown reason. She stared at me from across the room in my math teacher Mrs. Tyson's seventh grade class. Mrs. Tyson wore polyester clothes and had oily hair. Okay, it was the seventies and everyone was wearing polyester but her oily hair was her very own fashion.

Mrs. Tyson thought that I did not deserve to be skipped a grade because I was not very good at math. Still am not.

No, I wasn't good at math, but I could read anyone under the table, so there. I was smart but not a show-off about it. Scored in the ninety-ninth percentile on those standardized tests. And with the exception of Mrs. Tyson, I was a teacher's pet. They loved me. They really loved me. Teachers sometimes aren't really fair. If you make them feel like they are capable and good because you actually get what they are saying, you are their best friend for life.

I was also well-behaved and obedient. Oh, those were the days.

Melinda. She wore glasses. I did, too. They were some horrible red/brown aviator type. Well, Melinda's glasses were too small for her face. She had to tilt them down and rest them on the edge of her nose like some old lady because the handles could not fit conformably behind her ears. She wore high-water pants, and her clothes were too small.

If my clothing cut off my circulation, I guess I'd be pissed, too.

Gosh, there was no real reason for anyone to be so angry with me. I was no beauty queen and always bore the brunt of many fat jokes.

When she'd snarl, "Meet you after school." I'd be nervous but not too much. I had an escape plan. Like clockwork, my father met me after school at the end of the block in that maroon Plymouth station wagon. I made sure that I was in the front of the line, leaving me a few steps ahead of that ass whipping. I'd run down the hill to the car, hoping to get in before she could get to me. As I jumped into the car, I'd look up the block only to see Melinda heading in the opposite direction towards the housing projects.

And so it went. I didn't know if or when it was going to occur. I stuck to my plan anyway, just in case my luck ran out. My father was totally unaware of my dilemma. He, wearing his cashmere overcoat or tan raincoat, and a bit too much cologne, was far too preoccupied with getting to his job on time.

So that's how it went for me. So it surprises even me that I would even cavort with the likes of Tanya. I guess I shouldn't be surprised really. I am always up for an adventure and I try to keep an open mind, often convincing myself that things, or people, are not so bad. Judge not and thou shall not be judged. I just can't resist getting biblical.

And anyway, she made me become more aware of my own negative thoughts. Like, "I'm never going to get out of here," and "Why am I here in the first place?" Stuff like that. She was like my own little personal New Age guru wrapped in evangelical clothing.

When I started getting negative, she'd just give me that look — the one with her eyebrows raised and eyes wide open, glaring. A "don't you dare go there" kind of thing. And I would stop obediently in my tracks and rephrase the statement in the positive. I'd say things like, "Yes, I love it here. I'm having a wonderful time. It's God's will."

Her eyebrows would lower and she'd give a nod in the affirmative. Yes, tough love, laced with intimidation, is life transforming.

One day, she shared that she had been in jail overnight for stabbing a man and slashing his tires.

"Did I tell you," she said, "I was in jail?"

No, I don't think I would have forgotten something like that. It's not every day that I meet someone with a felony arrest at an upscale gym. The only thing that kept her out of the state penitentiary was that the victim failed to show up in court and they were obliged to drop the case.

I kind of took the stabbing in stride, as well as later tidbits, or shall I say, bombs she dropped on me.

When she dropped these whoppers, the conversation would usually begin, "Didn't I tell you about . . . ?"

"No," I would say, trying not to flinch.

She promised me she had reformed. She admitted back then "she was nothing nice." She found God in that jail cell, and it changed her life. I guess there is no conversion like a jailhouse conversion. Nothing like going to the bathroom in full view of everyone and hearing the moans of people sleeping on the cold cement floor to bring you closer to Jesus.

She may have found God, but she had not completely lost her edge. The genteel folks in the gym said that they admired and respected Tanya's honesty. Oh, she was honest alright. She'd tell you about yourself to your face. Pants too tight? She'd tell you. Put on a few pounds? She'd tell you about that, too. Need to marry that man you've been sleeping with for years. Oh she'd let you know, hand on her hip, pointing that long manicured finger in your face.

Where do I find these people? Or better yet, where do they find me?

Never mind.

So when Tanya told me about her church, I listened. Hell, if it can change a hard-boiled sister like her, who knows what it could do for me?

She told me that she saw a demon cast out of a man once right there in the midst of the service. He was thrashing about, talking shit. (My word, of course, not hers. In her conversion, she also gave up the use of profanity. That's deep.)

Bam, alacazam. The hands were laid, the words were spoken, and that demon was sent packing. Wow. Maybe I can learn a thing or two. Knowledge like that could come in quite handy, for I always feel like I am fighting the forces of evil.

I remember my first experience with church in the South. I was visiting my grandmother when I was four, five or something like that. Dressed in a white heavily starched dress, patent leather shoes, with short socks with frills around the ankles, I was taken to some white wooden building and dropped off to learn about Jesus and such under the tutelage of what seemed to be a very tall, heavily browed, brown-skinned woman.

There was a window in the room that seemed a little too small to jump out of. I must admit there wasn't much I remembered about that day. I'm sure there were other children in the room, but I sensed it was no time to start making friends. There was a problem about to erupt that would require my full attention.

The Sunday school teacher began going around the room asking children to recite Bible verses.

Bible verses. I'm sure I had learned how to read only a few months earlier and this . . . woman . . . was expecting me to recite a Bible verse.

Well, all the children gladly piped in, reciting their favorite verse like little automatons. Then she came around to me.

"(Blah, blah) Bible verse (blah, blah)," she said. I always had a hard time trying to understand the native tongue.

I just stared. I really didn't understand the meaning of "Bible verse." It wasn't in the Catholic lexicon.

She said it again this time with a snarl in her voice, "(Blah, blah, blah) Bible verse."

There I was, still staring, eyes wider than ever, shaking in my patent leathers.

The top of her head looked like it was about to blow off when she shouted, "Jesus wept!"

"Excuse me?" I asked.

"Say, Jesus wept!!" she screamed, steam coming from her ears.

I heard her loud and clear that time.

"Jesus wept," I said meekly. And I sat down in a pool of my own sweat.

I always seemed to be on the other side of some great religious divide. Catholics like me, are like heretics in this part of 'Bama. Strange people with even stranger practices.

Folks in need of a good conversion.

My Alabama grandmother despised Catholics. Well, she never came right out and said it, but I knew she did. Evidence: When my mother wanted to join the local Catholic church located behind their home, she told her flat out "No." Reason: She would not be able to go to church every Sunday so she would start out sinning. Lame excuse if ever I heard one. Everyone knows that not all Catholics go to mass every Sunday, right? We all can't be going to hell, right?

During one visit to Grandma's house when I was older if not wiser, I was cooking some bologna in a frying pan when from out of nowhere, my grandmother let me have it: "Why do you think that the Pope's unfailable?"

What? Maybe she meant "infallible"? Whatever.

"And why do you pray to Mary?" she asked.

What?

As always, another unnamed relative would pipe in with his two cents, providing her with an inspiring Amen corner.

Bewildered, I said nothing. I knew when she got started that I couldn't win. I am no scripture scholar and I wasn't about to defend the Catholicism especially not without ample ammunition. I'd say one thing and then she'd hit me with a barrage of Bible verses.

So, many years later and a couple years after Grandma met her maker, I met Mary, a student in one of my Intro to Communications courses and a devout Catholic.

Mary wanted to become a nun. There was just one minor problem. She was married with children. This little stumbling block did little to dissuade her.

Being a nun was great, but Mary had her eyes on a bigger prize. Sainthood.

Yes, I said sainthood.

When Mary disclosed her heavenly ambitions to the class, we all laughed. She didn't. She was dead serious.

"Doesn't every Catholic want to become a saint and/or a nun?" she asked innocently.

No. I set my sights high but not that high.

Mary was unapologetically Catholic. Every one of the required presentations for class had a Catholic theme. We got used to it after awhile.

She even gave us a test to determine if we should explore a career in the vocations.

In a darkened classroom with pens and pencils in hand, we took the test. Eight questions in all with two choices of responses, yes or no. We toiled away for all of two minutes.

"Everyone finished?" she asked.

We nodded.

Then she asked, "Anyone answer 'yes' to more than three questions?"

I proudly raised my hand. I looked around. Two others had their hands raised. Not good.

"Then you are a good candidate for the vocations," she said.

Noooooo!!! I was distracted for the rest of the class, my mind tormented by thoughts of habits of the long, black, penguin-looking kind.

I pulled Mary aside after class.

"What does this all mean?" I asked, my voice cracking.

"It means that you should explore becoming a member of the vocations. I have to go," she said as she scurried off.

"Don't go," I shouted if only in my mind. I can't become a nun. Austerity is not my strong suit. I love clothes and cursing too much. How dare she leave me this way?

Mary knew her stuff. She would have given my grandmother a run for her money.

Experiencing Mary was wonderful, but I had done the Catholic thing for so long, I could say the mass in a coma. I decided that it was time for a change.

I had heard of Tanya's church. Even saw them on television. They looked great — a kind of interracial, funkified thing not normally found in these parts. It's either black or white, not black and white.

There was a group singing on a platform in front of a full

band and choir. The tunes had a good beat. Not a finger-snapping, head-nodding beat, more like a toe-tapping one. A chronic channel zapper, I did not tune in long enough to hear the sermon but, from what I had seen, I knew they could put on a good show.

I eventually visited the church and discovered that it was run by a casual/shirt-wearing, head-mic-wearing, white-haired white man too hip for his own good.

Services took place in a renovated theater. The large projection screens above our heads flashed announcements and song lyrics just in case you wanted to sing along. Congregants sat in the round on the type of cream-colored chairs usually found in a banquet room. The people were friendly but not too much so. I soon discovered that this wonderfully integrated congregation did not exist in reality. It was really majority black, about eighty-five percent.

There was a come-as-you-are kind of atmosphere. I was digging that. I hate to dress up, but I couldn't get into wearing jeans to church, which many did.

The services began with at least forty minutes of singing to make sure we were really "in the spirit."

It looked so much better on television. Doesn't everything?

My shoes were either too tight or too loose, and I was always way to tired. If we didn't start holding up our arms and swaying appropriately to music, the pastor would cue the band to play yet another song.

Perhaps the rapture, hands raised high, swaying to and fro, and talking in "tongues" — a language only known by God — was supposed to help us forget — lose our minds, so to speak — if but for a little while. We could forget about that overdue bill, that boyfriend who hasn't called in a week, that jackass of a boss. No, we weren't in heaven but a close facsimile. And if you didn't feel it, you were encouraged by both the pastor and his rather gruff wife to fake it. You'd feel it eventually.

They never said what religion they were. Tanya told me that "Pastor" didn't believe in religion. It's not in the Bible.

And there weren't any members, just "attendees." I bought it for a time. But after awhile, it did begin to bother me. No members means no board members. And no board members means no accountability.

I received a newsletter from them. It didn't list any missions or volunteer opportunities. Oh yeah, they did make a call for singers and television camera operators.

Tanya said that they were Bible based but the minister never read more than a half of a verse of scripture at any given service. I wondered about the other two or three words left in the line. Didn't they have any meaning?

When I tried to express my reservations to Tanya, I was told not to question a man of God. Quite surprising coming from the likes of a bold woman like her. But there's very little in life that seems to make sense to me.

Like I said, I played along for a while. I even purchased my very own Bible to take with me to the service, not that we used it all that much. My Bible wasn't the fancy leather-bound kind with my name embossed on gold on the front. And it was not the kind that was so annotated or loosely interpreted that it had Jesus serving up barbecue matzos at the Last Supper. It was a paperback. The New International Version, also known as NIV. And it cost a reasonable six dollars and ninety-nine cents.

And like all churches, the pastor preached tithing. Give if you got it. Give if you don't. As it's presented, it's like signing up for the spiritual gambling. I put my money on God, double or nothing.

It was my last stop on my quest to find a church home. Church home? That's what they call it in 'Bama. When you meet someone for the first time, they don't ask about your background, education, or dreams but about your church home. "Do you have one? Are you looking for one?"

The love affair didn't last. They never do.

I had sampled some from the Baptist, Methodist, and although I had become a bit weary, even the Catholic. Yeah, I attended a Catholic church, the likes of which I had never seen before.

It was a black Catholic church complete with a Kwanzaa ceremony, gospel choir, and liturgical dancers. Most Sundays I wasn't quite sure where I was. I heard a whole lot of spontaneously spoken "amens" and other Protestant-like mumblings.

You'd think I'd feel comfortable with this hybrid since I was christened Baptist and baptized Catholic. (This shouldn't surprise you.) But I like my Catholicism served straight up, no fancy stuff. I like my masses to begin on time and end in an hour. This particular priest, a homegrown 'Bama boy — nice guy — grew up not too far from my grandmother and had a penchant for starting late and ending late.

The gospel choir was okay. I always love a good concert. But I often wondered if they knew that this was very unusual and not very Catholic. The mass is supposed to be a meditation — a time for reflection on the goodness of God, not that kick-ass solo by Mrs. Jones.

In all fairness, there was one thing good about the church. On the grounds was a home for severely disabled children and adults. My aunt worked there many years ago. I visited once. Children, whose necks couldn't bear the weight of their heads, sat idly, glass-eyed and drooling. I wasn't afraid, just sad.

The children and adults from the facility attended mass. They sat in wheelchairs along the side aisles where they moaned or perhaps tried to speak.

Church offered a respite from their lives — a place to be with a God who seems to have all but abandoned them. No one ever talked to them save their caretakers. When I walked past them after having received communion, I always tried to look at them and smile. I'm not sure if they noticed really or even cared. I needed to do it, not necessarily for them, but for me.

When the service hit the two-and-half-hour mark, thanks to a presentation of officers and other happenings, I had had enough.

I was such a lousy Catholic. I thought maybe I would make a better Jew. I was often fascinated by the religion and the culture. I knew a little about Judaism, having been born and raised in New York. My mother once brought home a book on the Jewish holidays, and I read a bit of it. I also attempted to make a documentary on black Jews, the Falashas, and people with combined black and Jewish heritage. I even wrote articles on Chanukah and Passover for Montgomery's newspaper supplement.

For my Chanukah article, I visited a kindly young rabbi at the conservative temple in town. A diminutive young man with a pale face and a high-pitched staccato voice, he invited me into his office to chat and to play a friendly game of the dreidle game.

I love games. I'm not really competitive, but I do hate to lose.

He explained the rules and handed me my own plastic orange dreidle to play with. The pot was colorful hard candy.

He allowed me to go first. I spun it. The dreidle went round and round and the landed on "hey." I took half of the pot.

It was the rabbi's turn. He spun his dreidle. It landed on "nun." He gets nothing. My turn.

I spun. It landed on "gimel." Good golly, I got it all. It was mine, all mine, every last tooth-rotting little piece.

It seems somewhat sinful to have gotten so much pleasure beating someone, especially a holy man. He took it well, thank God.

At the request of a friend, I attended a Shabbat service at the reformed temple. I was a bit nervous standing there in the midst of the other congregants. There was always so much ink and airtime given to the tension between blacks and Jews that I thought that my mere presence would start a riot.

It didn't.

The service was so soothingly familiar with its chant-like singing and orderly progression of things it reminded me of the traditional mass.

Who would have thought that I would learn more about the Jewish race, religion, and culture while living in the South? It's interesting that Jews spend a lifetime trying to remember, while the rest of us spend a lifetime trying to forget.

Alas, I had to admit, conversion was not the answer.

That turned out to be the last stop for me. No more aimless wanderings through the world of churching.

So, I sat at home Sunday mornings, watching church in the box.

Perhaps this acute dissatisfaction with organized religion comes from the knowledge that I don't have to be in a church or belong to a church to have a relationship with God. I found God in all the usual places — in my classroom and in the quiet moments early in the morning when the only sound heard is that of my own breathing, letting me know that I am here to live the promise of yet another day.

That's it. It's over between us.

. . . For now.

Breaking Chains

Remember this if nothing else: God is a God of second chances.

I'm not a coward. I don't let fear get the best of me. Strange places and even stranger people are a challenge — something to be explored. So why was I so hesitant about visiting Julia Tutwiler prison?

I knew no one inside. When folks talked about their relatives in lock-down as if all we black people shared this common bond, I politely smiled. My people guard the prisoners; they are not the prisoners themselves.

I was afraid. And I didn't know of what.

My imagination ran wild. Maybe the inmates would be like those tough girls in the other class in grade school. The class that wasn't so smart, or so the teachers told them. The class that didn't get the nice new shiny books and whose clothes were a bit worn. Angry at the world and taking it out on you. They dared you to look directly in their eyes — demanding to know what you are staring at.

So you held your head down, in fear and shame, and you walked a wide berth around them in the hallway or on the playground, forcing you to feel in that moment the shame and self-consciousness they felt every day of their lives.

A month or so earlier, I had signed on as a volunteer for

an inmate mothers' group. I wasn't just any volunteer but a board member. I didn't have to work hard to get my lofty position. I was at a function at the fine cultural institution, munching on way too many crackers and cheese cubes, my feet aching from standing on the cold, hard, tile floor when one of our volunteers approached me, a diminutive woman with a big personality,

"Do you want to become a board member for _____?" she asked.

Board member? How often does one get such an invitation? I knew board members yielded great power which I observed during my stay at the cultural institution. I don't care what books you have read or what some bleeding heart has told you, power is a good thing.

"Let me think about it," I said cooly, sipping on my Dixie cup full of soda.

I thought about it for two seconds and called her within two days. I filled out the appropriate papers, talked to the appropriate people. My name and credentials were presented to the other board members for a vote and bam, I was in — in charge. Of what, I wasn't quite sure.

The experience was lovely. Nothing too taxing or taking me out of my comfort zone. A meeting here. A meeting there. I could convince myself that serving as a volunteer for a prisoner advocacy group was a lovely, sanitized experience. But I could not hide forever. Yeah, yeah, I read the literature. I knew that although violent offenders are housed at Tutwiler, many of the women were in for nonviolent offenses ranging from shoplifting to grand theft and robbery. It didn't matter, I was still afraid.

But I'm not a coward. And I set out to prove it.

I gathered the courage to contact Jean, the executive director, to sign up to help with the monthly prison visits wherein kids and moms get together or the monthly storybook project, wherein inmates tape recorded books and messages to send to their children. Good ole Jean had something else in mind, nothing so nice. Jean wanted me to sit in on the domestic violence focus group.

In the days leading up to my visit, I thought not only about the inmates I would meet but also about domestic violence or "DV" as the professionals called it.

As a small child, I witnessed violent acts perpetrated against my mother's female friends by their husbands.

Bruised and battered, these strong, comforting women, working both at home and on the job, went on with their lives. As fate would have it, one husband was found dead of complications caused by chronic alcoholism. Yet another's life of violence and irrationality led him, a driver for a municipal bus system, to shoot a passenger following a verbal altercation, leading to his arrest and conviction.

After seeing these random acts of violence, I vowed, as many young children do, that such a thing would never happen to me and comforted myself with the conviction that I would have a plan of action and the means to execute it.

In 1970s America, we were just beginning to understand the concept of what we call domestic violence. In earlier years, many thought the beatings and berating were rites of passage. I would come to learn that, for the women of Alabama, little had changed.

A few days before the visit, I was briefed about the rules I had to follow. Although I am not a rules kind of girl, I knew had to comply.

No jewelry. No shorts. No sleeveless shirts. No sneakers. Don't wear white. Only carry into the prison your keys and driver's license.

The trip to Tutwiler from Montgomery was uneventful and rather soothing. The winding, tree-lined roads along Highway 231 weren't crowded out by too many strip malls, fast food places, and drive-thru banks. I allowed my mind to wander aimlessly; so much so that I thought I had passed the place. I stopped twice, once at a gas station and the next time at a propane store.

"I'm looking for Julia Tutwiler Prison. Have I passed it?"

"Keep going," they said.

"You can't miss it," they said.

They were right. Before I knew it, seemingly out of nowhere loomed the massive white exterior of Julia Tutwiler prison in the foreground with its white cinderblock and brick and distinctive, characteristic barbed wire. I parked in front of the building, my car skidding on the gravel. I made a last check of everything and realized I was still wearing my watch. I opened the glove compartment and tossed it in. I really can't say the prison wasn't like what I had imagined because I'd never imagined that I would be visiting a prison.

Once inside, I approached the female corrections officer sitting behind a Plexiglas counter complete with metal bars. She neither smiled nor spoke. Grunted and snarled was more like it. I knew the rules and handed over my identification and keys.

I looked around the waiting room. Nothing fancy. Not the bright white of outside but a rather dullish color, ecru maybe. It looked like so many other waiting rooms in government facilities.

Another female corrections officer approached me.

"Step into the bathroom," she said pointing in the direction of a closed door near the front and motioned for me to starting heading there.

I began walking — not too fast, not too slow. She followed my every move. Once inside, I was instructed to take off my shoes and turn around. Terribly germ-phobic, I get creeped out by the smallest of things, and having to stand on that cold tile floor nearly sent me over the edge. Thank God I wore tights. And I can still feel, under my feet, the groves separating each tile. I was asked to turn around and raise my arms. My heart raced and jaw clenched. As she patted me down, I could feel my fear turning into anger and righteous indignation. How dare she, I'm no criminal. I found the invasion of privacy intolerable, and I had only been there for a few minutes.

When she finished, I exhaled and put on my shoes.

I was a changed woman. Angry at the system.

When I reentered the waiting room, Jean and three representatives from the Alabama Coalition Against Domestic Violence had finally arrived. We proceeded through the big, white, heavy, metal, gate. The sound of it closing behind us seemed to ring out — haunting. I was truly on the other side. No escaping.

We met one of the inmates — a friendly older black woman, who shook our hands as she introduced herself. She decided to give us a tour of the arts and crafts room. We didn't ask for one, nor did we refuse her offer. She took us to the break room, where women were milling about as they tried to gather a group to do a little exercise. I couldn't tell if they were paying much attention to us. I was back in school again, looking down, trying to avoid eye contact.

We followed the woman as she took us to another room. At the far end sat two diminutive older women, one black and one white. They talked about their work — making stuffed rabbits — as they sewed on the ears. The inmates invited us to return in a couple of weeks to view the finished product. Other handcrafts were on display, including a crocheted Halloween doll and leather handbags, including one which read, "#1 Mother."

Tour finished, we went into the hallway and waited.

While Jean gathered the inmates together, the representatives and I stood in the hallway. As the inmates moved about, I observed their different shapes, sizes, and colors. I also noticed that I was quite relaxed.

Finally, the group gathered in a small room — twelve inmates, Jean, the shelter reps, and I. The space was cramped to say the least, no air conditioning and no windows. All the women wore their white cotton suits with faded numbers on the breast pocket.

A coalition representative from East Alabama explained the purpose of the focus group was to gather information that would help the program directors better tailor their program to the women's needs so that the women would not end up in prison.

Some of the inmates were graduates of the program's domestic violence workshop, which helps domestic violence survivors deal with the issues surrounding their abuse. A popular program, it can only accommodate seventeen participants per session, and there is always a waiting list.

Many of the inmates were serving time for crimes resulting from domestic violence. Unlike the women I knew growing up, these women struck back. Although everyone's story was undoubtedly different, as I had anticipated, the inmates shared one shocking commonality — with the exception of one woman, none of them used the services of domestic violence shelters. In fact, they were neither informed by the doctors who treated them (only three were treated by physicians) nor by law enforcement of their availability.

The women were sharp and open for questions and comments. As in any group, some spoke more than others. The most vocal was a petite, fast-talking women named Jennifer. The only one who sought refuge in a shelter, she stated that it took her two days to be admitted into the facility. Once there, she said that she was asked numerous and seemingly invasive questions. She felt that her confidentiality would be breached and her whereabouts revealed.

The representative explained that the questions were necessary, in part to satisfy the needs of the shelters' funders who needed a significant amount of documentation and numerous reports. Also, the statistics can be used to help the community become more aware of the growing need for more facilities. But, she explained, hearts are seldom moved, and shelters rarely built — the not-in-my-backyard syndrome was in full effect.

The inmates were shocked by attitude of the communities, leaving one to blurt out, "Are you telling us that communities feel safe when we are getting beat up and abused?"

Imagine living in a rural area, you and your husband go at it or, rather, he goes at you. He takes the car, your only means of transportation. You're in the middle nowhere, face bleeding, and heart aching. You start out on foot, but halfway down the road you stop. You realize you have nowhere to go. You want to move forward, but you know you have to turn back. How would you feel?

The problem is that most people don't bother to think much less feel.

I knew life was unfair but I was made painfully aware how unfair. It's a man's world when it comes to DV. According to the representative, most men don't serve any time for domestic violence abuses. Judges often give them deferred or suspended sentences. Many are ordered to attend domestic violence intervention programs. As often happens, once the abuser's obligation is met, it's considered time served and/or the charges are dismissed.

If nothing is done and the woman strikes back, it's usually with the same or greater level of violence as her aggressor used against her. I can only imagine. Enough is enough, and she reaches for the nearest weapon, a gun, a knife, or some other object. She swings, shoots, jabs, and she makes contact. He slows down. More contact. He stops, falters, and falls. She stands over him and shoots, jabs, and hits again, and again, and again, each bullet hole, cut, and bruise for every time he hit her in front of her children; belittled her; made her feel stupid, ugly, and worthless. Before she realizes it, he is seriously or mortally wounded. How did it go so wrong? She didn't want to kill him. She only wanted him to stop.

When the session was over, the some of the women cleared the room, some of us remained. We had to wait for Jean, who'd left to take care of some business. In the corner, sat Pamela. I went over to her. We chatted a bit. She told me that her son had been killed and that she had not seen her twenty-three-year-old daughter since her incarceration. The entire time, she was pleasant and had a slight smile. She concluded that in spite of everything, she was blessed. Blessed. How could she say she was blessed? The word is bandied about by televevanglists, and "Christians." Blessed to suffer. Blessed to know the pain of having to live yet another day separated from the world and those you love. It never ceases to amaze me how some people can find peace and grace amid some of life's most difficult circumstances.

These women could have been my family friends. Unlike those friends, impulse led them to strike back out of anger and frustration, their fate sealed behind iron bars.

I went back to the prison several times after that. I became determined to let the state if not the world know that prison life had a far-reaching effect. I wrote two op-eds, one for the *Montgomery Advertiser*, the other for the *Birmingham News*, asking for understanding while not condoning illegal behavior. If they do the crime, they must do the time, but to isolate these women from families, especially their young children during their most formative years, is truly criminal, and we all end up paying the price in higher rates of recidivism and the inevitable delinquency of those emotionally and physically abandoned children.

I knew of one girl, now a woman, full of rage, against an enemy known only to her, she picked fights with everyone who dared look at her too hard or too long. Her mother had done time, in that same prison, for one year, but one year in a child's life is like a century. She survived having missed an appointment with generational history. Most aren't so lucky.

I went on with the business of being a board member, attending meetings and such. One uneventful afternoon, we met. We were winding down the order of business, eating generic chips and cookies, drinking soda from plastic cups. The fare was paltry compared to the offering at the cultural institution where even the most mundane meetings are catered affairs. I didn't care that the offerings weren't glamorous; we were working for a higher cause, a loftier ideal.

One pressing matter we had to attend to was a vote to hire

Bess, an ex-con out on parole, as a rehabilitation specialist, a person who would help the women transition from inside to outside. All hands were raised. The vote was unanimous, Bess would be hired. Why not, she did her time, a second chance should be allowed.

My vote for Bess was one of the high points of my tenure. The politics of position made it nearly impossible to affect widely sweeping change. As always, I was on the other side of a great divide.

I was able to do a few things. I created a survey fleshing out the interests and capabilities of board members and recruited a valuable board member who helps with the Storybook Project. And I organized an exhibition of prisoner artwork, got the local paper to promote it, and one of the works sold to a local defense attorney.

I wanted to do more but was unable to.

I finally got to meet Bess in person at a going away party for one of the staff members. She was a tall, chocolate woman with short hair, more salt than pepper, who looked like a beloved young grandma or an older auntie. Not an ex-con. Quietly, she ate, only responding to our occasional questions. She had children; they were all doing well. She had used the system to educate herself and held numerous certificates. Bess made a daily commute to work from Birmingham, where she stayed to care for her ailing father. But that day, mostly she watched and listened as the presents were opened and the goodbyes and good lucks said to the Americorp staffer.

Fast forward to a year and a half later. I was doing a radio talk show and I needed to fill a spot on the day after Thanksgiving. Brainstorm. Bess. Yeah. A couple of months earlier, I had Jean on to talk about the organization and asked her if Bess was ready and willing to tell her story. She told me that Bess had already gotten out there. I called Bess. She agreed to do it and called me, "precious" which is even better than "pretty."

So, very nervous, Bess came to the studio on that rainy

post-Thanksgiving morning, and was greeted by me and my bombastic co-host.

"You all have to help me get through this; I have never done this before," she said, her voice trembling.

Before he could go on about his extensive radio experience, blah, blah, blah, I quickly said, "Don't worry. You will do great."

And she did. A few pre-interview questions before we went on the air loosened her up. And she told her story in a clear and steady voice for all the area to hear. She had been in for forgery, serving a life sentence under the three strike rule. Bess did some time in with the feds, nearly two years, and the rest, about seven, she did with the state. She was the only daughter of a Pentecostal minister, and her mother suffered from mental illness. And it was her father's name that she forged on the loan application that sent her up for the long stint.

When they met in court, she and her dad, Bess was sure that he was going to bail her out like he had done so many times before. She was his baby, a true daddy's girl, traveling with him from church to church.

She said he looked at her and said, "I leave you in God's hands."

So, at an age when most people are contemplating the end of the journey, retirement, a life of casual contemplation, and relaxation, she was locked up in lock-down — for life. She described being very hungry early on in her stay, with dinner served in the mid-afternoon and not having earned any money to purchase snacks. Bess also had a world of time to think about what she had done. With every action restricted, the only thing she could do was endure.

I asked her why someone like her, the daughter of minister, would commit such a crime, and more importantly, why others with similar backgrounds, do the same.

"Because they can get away with," she said. "It's like a rush."

A rush? I may drive five miles (okay, ten) above the speed limit, but I'm plagued with too much Catholic guilt to do something truly illegal.

Nearly a year later, I had lunch with Mama Bess, which is what the prisoners had called her. It was one of our last meetings. I told her I wanted to write a book about her life. She had a story to tell and I wanted to tell it. Perhaps the publicity could generate additional money for her projects, which included purchasing computers for the women. She agreed.

It never happened. The book, that is. We know about what can happen to the best laid plans. She was too busy and seemed to become disinterested. Our final conversation on the matter was brief. After she had unceremoniously stood me up, I gave her a call. I had selected some dates for us to meet. She was too busy rattling off meeting after meeting, engagement after engagement.

Sensing my growing anxiety, she said, "Don't give up on me."

It was too late. I already had.

But the lunch meeting that day was full of hope. We sat in the dark booth and ate mushroom burgers with Swiss cheese, my favorite. I was a gooey mess. Too much ketchup and mustard caused the condiments to ooze over the sides of the bun and cover my hands with a delectable ketchup/mustard mixture. I had to wipe and wipe with every available napkin and still act like I was graceful and somewhat well-mannered. Always too thirsty, I downed sodas as fast as the waitress could refill my glass.

I asked Bess about her father, now a victim of both Alzheimer's and Parkinson's diseases.

"He has good days and bad days," she said resolutely. She and her daughter, a nurse, shared in his care.

She gave me more details about the final forgery that landed her in prison. She had signed her father's name to a $20,000 loan. She had to pay her father restitution out of her meager earnings. It was a kick in the head going to her father's mailbox and seeing the check, the restitution money.

And she didn't take the money for herself but to help someone else in need.

You know me, I had to ask, "I was just wondering Bess, did your father turn you in?"

"No, he didn't. It was the bank that went after me," said Bess.

"Wouldn't he have given you the money anyway, if you had asked?"

She smiled at the irony, "He probably would have. It was his fault, you know; he always told me not to ask, just take what I wanted."

I wanted to say, "Come on, Bess," but I let it slide.

In class at the university, someone asked about the criminality of writing bad checks. I didn't know the answer and told them I would ask Bess about it.

"Don't write checks without money in the bank," she said. She didn't even have a checking account, not trusting herself quite yet.

A penny short, it's still a bad check, so I was informed. You have ten days to make good. If you don't, your ass is going to jail, and your picture will be on the local news and your name in the newspaper.

"Don't do it. I can't help you if you go in. I can come and visit," she said.

We chatted about the book, which she thought was a great idea, and invited me to hear her speak at Maxwell AFB on behalf of the United Way Campaign. I was delighted.

I traveled to Maxwell, on the other side of town. Montgomery is a military town, two bases, Maxwell and Gunter. Many people are either retired military, children of military dependents who decided to retire in Montgomery, or just plain ole served in somebody's war.

The post 9/11 security was tight. Nervously, I drove up to the guard shack. Two young men, one white, one black, in their uniformed best, manned the booth.

"I'm here for the United Way Campaign. I should be on the list."

I waited as they perused the list.

"It's in the activities center. You can go through," they said.

Probably for the first time in my driving life, I followed the speed limit. Slowly and carefully, I made my way through to the center. The base was quiet in a rather idyllic way with its manicured lawns and little Americana houses.

Inside the activities center, there were tables with information from the various United Way Agencies — people with smiles, good clothes, and inviting eyes manning them.

An older black gentleman with salt-and-pepper hair approached me. I guess I looked lost.

Before he could say a word, I blurted out, "I'm here to hear Bess Douglas. She invited me," I said.

He escorted me to the front of the room and showed me where Bess would be sitting. I sat in the chair behind hers.

Men and women in uniform began to stream in. I craned my neck and looked around. No Bess. I waited impatiently.

I looked at the clock. Almost time and still no Bess. Finally, Bess entered carrying an armload of boxes.

She came over and gave me a big hug.

"It's so good to see you, precious," she said. My heart warmed.

She looked so regal in her blue suit. Our love fest didn't last long; she had to greet the media. A cameraman was waiting to interview her for a local news broadcast. She was poised and ready. Bess had come a long way.

We heard many stories that day. The opener was a real tear-jerker.

Finally, it was Bess' turn to speak.

She began her story. I had heard most of it before. But to hear her speak before the crowd in a clear and powerful voice, gave it deeper meaning. Bess told how, while incarcerated, she had participated in the services provided by the prison advocacy organization just for the hot dogs and the change of pace but, later, she became hooked.

Her voice cracked only once — when she spoke about her father. She said that God blessed her, allowing her to get out of prison in time to care for him the way he had cared for her.

Tired of taking, she wanted to give back. It had become her life's goal.

Quiet. No fidgeting or ruffling of papers. All eyes were on Bess. I tried not to cry. I felt like a proud mama bear, I knew how far Bess had come and I saw her future in Technicolor. There was a pause after the presentation, then a round of applause.

People swarmed around Bess afterwards. A long line formed just to thank her, to shake her hand, with some asking what they could do to help.

True redemption is possible.

A Double-Wide Life

The most difficult shackles to lose are those that chain the mind.

Tammy was a dishwater blond, a color too fair for her complexion and clearly applied by untrained or poorly trained hands. With blond being the one true thing, natural or not, I guess it didn't really matter.

Tammy was funny.

Her stories had an energy, a vibrancy, a bounce that garnered not the slight chuckle that usually lasts for only a couple of seconds but a belly laugh deep down that lingers for days and make the abs much more sore than sit-ups. Your eyes water. You are out of breath. And afterwards, you feel good, cleansed. You know I'm not one to laugh at just anything; so you know this girl was good.

I remember thinking she looked a little fat, sitting there in one of the rounded soft, chairs in the cultural institution's reception area, wearing her dingy white cotton sweater. In Alabama, big bellies are not an uncommon sight.

I dare not ask someone if she's pregnant. It's just one of the cardinal sins. I know you feel tempted sometimes, thinking that they'll understand if you make a mistake. They won't. I don't care if their belly is sticking out a mile in front of them. Don't ask, please. I say this for your own good.

She was waiting to take her place at the front desk to answer the nonringing phone. The head guy insisted that we man the phone during the spring festival — a day-long event held on the cultural institution's grounds. All hands had to be on deck. For our efforts, we got a couple of hot dogs, a banana, and some chips, and the satisfaction of a job done, if we were lucky, well done.

I was upstairs taking a break, trying to escape the heat. My assignment: taking photos of the fun.

It was a good day. I had my picture taken with Ronald McDonald for posterity. It was at his insistence, I swear.

I hung the picture on my cubicle wall. I looked thin. He looked like . . . Ronald.

So there we were, Tammy and I, sitting chatting, whining, and moaning.

And Tammy says, "Blah, blah, blah . . . I'm five months pregnant."

What?

Maybe I said, "Well, congratulations." But "That's nice" seems more like it.

Questions began sprinting through my head like some rabbit on speed. Like, for example, who's the baby's daddy? Are you married to the baby's daddy? Are you going to be on Springer? The usual nosey stuff.

Remember, however, I'm not nosey, just inquisitive.

Also running through my inquisitive brain was the question: Whom should I ask these questions? It certainly wasn't going to be her. How rude would that have been?

I knew she was good friends with Eve. My girl Eve. She looked like singer Pink's much-heavier first cousin with a round face and attitude for days. From her behavior, I sensed that she had been around a chocolate person or two in her day. Darling, white people aren't born with the shit to be the shit. It's acquired after much honest, up close, personal exposure. Watch all the BET you want; it's not going to happen. As it turned out, Eve's estranged husband was black and her two children biracial. I knew it.

A little Dominican girl from Inwood in NYC once told me when I asked how she could so easily tell the difference between a Dominican, a Puerto Rican, and a Cuban by just looking at them, "You know your people."

Since that moment, I have spent a great deal of time looking for my people, expecting to know them when I met them. It hasn't happened yet. Perhaps it's because the definition of "my people" is constantly in flux, taking some who were previously out, in, and leaving some who were previously in, out. Sometimes, I would look at my fellow brown-skinned folks and try to figure out whether they are Caribbean-American or African-American. Since I am a mix of both, I win either way.

The next day, I sat with Eve while she relieved the receptionist for lunch. I knew couldn't very well ask the baby daddy question in this oh-so-public place because the walls had ears, eyes, and a few teeth.

"Is Tammy married?" I asked innocently.

"No," she said.

"Oh," I said. "You know she is pregnant?"

"Yeah," she said matter-of-factly.

Damn, she's not giving up a thing, I thought. She had worked for the Feds — a military hospital in D.C. — prior to coming on board at the cultural institution. They taught her well. (She also worked at the state's health department. Her tales of STDs will make you want to wear a chastity belt and throw away the key.)

I decided to change the subject, to trip her up a bit.

"How's your daughter," I asked cheerily.

"Fine," she said and proceeded to tell me something that her chubby little one did. Eve's talking, but I'm hearing nothing but noise because I'm plotting my next strategy. It was scary and tough but I knew I had to go back in.

It was time for the surprise attack.

"What does the baby's father do?"

"Who?" she looked at me.

The phone rang. Damn.

Forget it. I decided to slink back to my desk. And wait. Keep my ears open, knowing somebody would break soon.

And someone did. The father was a doctor. Sorry, I can't reveal my sources.

Tammy claimed the pregnancy was a surprise to her.

Gee, I wonder what Santa will bring me this Christmas? No Santa? What a surprise.

Tammy kept getting bigger and bigger, and the day kept drawing nearer. We got tidbits about things here and there. Her sister-in-law had a bit of a criminal history, having sold Tupperware, kept the money for herself, and never delivered the plastic goods. Her parents were a tad wacky and very racist. They gave her turpentine and sugar to cure her of worms and considered the beloved sitcom "The Cosby Show," a nigger show.

Tammy herself held no ill will against people of color. She once had a black roommate and was a fan of 2 Live Crew. I'm okay with rap, but even I wouldn't go that far.

She'd recount her stories during one of those in-house mailings. And she made us laugh hard. I had nothing to contribute. My stories paled in comparison. I thought it was cool that she was able to laugh about the bad stuff.

My father was an alcoholic who forced me to make drinks for him and had a penchant for flying into drunken rages. I wish I could find the humor in it all. Perhaps if one can find the humor, one can find the healing there as well.

Tammy's stories were not quaint in a Rick Bragg sort of way. They were more like Billy Bob Thorton in *Sling Blade* — only a hair away from the evil that lurks within.

Bragg can afford to wax nostalgic about the South, for he was able to escape the cycle due to a combination of lucky breaks and talent. So many others left behind don't have the benefit of distance and dollars.

Tammy's condition became front office news. People at work love to gossip. Live for it. I'm inquisitive, but they are out and out nosey, pumping her directly for details. They didn't even have the grace to go behind her back. It would have been the Southern and hospitable thing to do. I was shocked at these older, proper churchgoing types with their noses in the air with all of their Southern good manners and grace.

"Did you know she was pregnant?"

"What is the world coming to?"

"Has she no shame?"

Now I know that the Bible doesn't condone gossip or meanness of any sort. I felt I had to defend her.

"She is a good person. Everyone makes mistakes."

They looked at me, humphed, and proceeded to go about their business.

They called her white trash behind her back. She lived in a trailer. So, what? My cousin used to live in a trailer park. My family, or shall I say my mother's family, never called it a trailer but a mobile home. The "mobile home" thing really threw me off. I just couldn't wrap my brain around that one. Black people don't live in trailers, or so I've been told. I never visited his home. Come to think of it, I was never invited.

I couldn't, wouldn't dare look down on her. Although we lived in a spacious Harlem apartment, we had our share of troubles with unwanted visitors (and I'm not talking about my relatives) and landlords who thought that heat and hot water were a luxury and not a necessity.

It didn't seem like she had much. Her parents were poor folks from Northern Alabama, and her siblings weren't doing much better. Then, I got a bright idea.

"We oughtta have a shower for her."

When I announced my plan, those gossipy women looked at me as if had spit in their faces.

I thought, okay, moving on.

I approached my boss; no, not true, supervisor of my department, not true either because she wasn't the boss of me or anyone else for that matter. The so-named department head — now that sounds right.

She thought it was a great idea and we took it to Tammy's supervisor, the Number Two Gal, who, to my surprise, agreed to host it at her home.

So we set a date, created invitations, and placed them in everyone's mailbox and went to Wal-Mart to buy gifts.

Well, when the pooh-poohers found out that the Number Two Gal was hosting, they had a sudden change of heart. Imagine that.

I wanted the day to be special. I made finger sandwiches, a fruit salad, and tuna fish sandwiches with the edges trimmed. I knew I was cooking. Somebody call Food TV.

I packed up the car, and with one hand on the food in the passenger seat and the other on the steering wheel, I was off to the Number Two Gal's house.

Tammy arrived with her sister, a delightful, older, petite brown-haired woman. There was plenty of food. And nearly everyone who was invited came. And those who couldn't or didn't come, sent presents. The Number Two Gal gave tours of her home. Everyone oohed and ahhed on cue. I didn't take the tour.

We sent everyone home with leftovers.

Hearts weren't completely melted but definitely softened.

There was going to be a new life filled with possibility and promise.

I was off that day but I heard about it. Tammy had a precious little girl — beautiful, a little over six pounds. Baby and mama were doing fine. I would have gone to the hospital, but I was afraid that I might run into her parents. Irrational, I know. What did I have to fear from a couple of old dried-up racists? What were they going to do, beat me with their walking sticks? I stayed away anyway.

After Tammy's baby was born, she invited me to come over her house to see the little thing. I had to go to Tammy's house. I gave her a shower and everything. You know Tammy lives in a trailer park. I hate the snooty part of myself. As much as I try to suppress it, it seeps through sometimes. I bucked up and convinced myself a trip to Tammy's house was just another adventure for me. Some people go to India. Others climb Mount Everest. I take a trip to a trailer park. You have your adventures; I have mine.

The excursion reminded me of the time when I had my friend Cassandra, a native of Los Angeles, drive me to see the black people in L.A. I knew they existed, I had even seen a few, but I wanted to go to the 'hood — that mythic place I had seen on the big screen and heard about in rap songs. You can imagine my joy when we stumbled upon a sea of black, brown, and high yella faces at the Black Family Reunion in South Central near the campus of USC. Popular in the nineties, it was the corporatization of the family reunion experience.

Tammy had given good directions. It was not too far from the mall, tucked away in a corner. I turned in onto the narrow street passed the single- and double-wides and found her trailer. Sprigs of grass tried to peek up from the mass of dirt in front of her house.

I was glad to see her. I got to see her little boo, slightly jaundiced and small with cute pudgy cheeks and a pug nose. And the trailer? It was okay. Nicely decorated. Baby toys, clothes, and paraphernalia everywhere. We watched television, talked, and I watched her care for her little one. I was confident that Tammy was going to make a great mom.

Not very long after the baby's birth, she left for a better-paying job with an opportunity for promotion. I hadn't heard from Tammy in awhile when one afternoon, a co-worker, a grunge type from Seattle, placed a copy of a news alert from the website of our local paper. It was a story about a baby being left in a hot car, windows rolled up, for an hour. An apartment manager found the baby and called 911. The mother in question had Tammy's name and age. The article said she was swimming in the pool, drunk, too drunk to tell police what had happened. They placed her under arrest.

Feeling personally responsible (I'll go into it later), I

couldn't stop shaking and crying. The baby nearly died. The thought of it unnerved me to my core.

The word started getting around. Was it true? Could it be true? No one wanted to think the worst.

My fears were confirmed when I saw her picture on the news, her name as clear as day. Glassy-eyed and barely recognizable, but I knew it was she. Alabama does the not-so-hospitable thing of plastering the faces of the accused, note: not convicted, across the television.

The story and photo ran at noon, five, six, ten, and the next day; and a piece appeared in the local paper.

How could it be? She loved that little girl.

Everyone at work was upset. We knew her personally. "What went wrong?" we asked ourselves. There were all kinds of theories, but none were confirmed or denied.

We loved that crazy gal and her baby. She didn't stay with us for very long, but she was family.

The media didn't know her. What happened to Tammy made me think of all of those post-tragedy interviews with friends and neighbors who say the same seemingly unbelievable things.

"He/she was a nice girl/boy, man/woman."

The viewers, listeners, readers, turn up their noses. They think to themselves, how could it be? Are they lying or living under a rock?

If the media asked us, we would have told them how she was a great mom — read to her girl nightly and spoke about her child with love in her eyes.

But nobody asked us.

Quickly, she lost her new fancy apartment, furniture, her job, and her daughter.

She called one day. I just picked up the phone at work and it was Tammy.

"Hey. How are you?"

"I'm doing good."

Tammy told me she had entered an alcohol treatment

program and found God.

I didn't feel like being nosey, just supportive.

"I love you Tammy, and I'm proud of you. Keep up the good work."

Later reports relayed that she had gone on with her life. She was attending college full-time and had no real thoughts of trying to regain custody.

Sometimes, I think, what was I thinking? I knew, we all knew, that she would eventually lose her precious daughter. She drank just a little too much. Liked to be out and about a little too much.

Maybe by giving her a baby shower, helping her out we just delayed the inevitable. Perhaps, if life had been hard enough for her, she would have seriously considered giving the baby up for adoption which would have been a true act of love.

She was stuck in a kind of pathology. Not only did she live in the trailer park, but the trailer park lived in her. Did we really think that introducing her to wine in a bottle, and crudités was going to change everything she was?

Like so many ghetto boys and girls, she, too, strived to keep it real.

As you know, I am plagued with the desire to fix things — cure things. I have come to realize that I don't do it for them but rather for me. I want to make everything nice and pretty, but sometimes life isn't so nice and pretty, and it needs to be that way.

Tammy had professional pictures taken to mark her baby's first Christmas. The little one was dressed in a red velvet dress with a white ruffle collar and sported a wide grin. Tammy gave me a photo. Gave all of us one who would take them. I still have that picture.

I also have a copy of the news report of her arrest, perhaps as a reminder that the fall from grace is swift.

One mistake can change a life for a lifetime.

back to a
beginning

Back to a Beginning

The road not taken is often a winding journey taking us back to a place where it all began.

Tired. I had a forty-five-minute break in between classes. Break? More like breather. I exhaled, snarfed down a Power-bar between classes as I sat at someone else's desk, not having my own because I was, after all, just an adjunct, an educator for hire. Did I say I was tired? No, I was way past tired, trying to juggle three jobs — the talk show hostess with the mostest, public relations maven of the very fine cultural institution, and teacher of all things somewhat relevant.

I made a phone call or two. My eye was on the clock overhead. I looked up: 12:55. The buzzer rang in my head — time to go for the second and final act of the dog and pony show.

The dog and pony show was clearly on its last legs. They meandered in. I was glassy eyed, and so were they, perhaps on a sugar low from lunch. Disinterested at best, they slouched in their chairs, placed their heads on their desks or stared out of the window.

The classroom was too small, seemed almost claustrophobic. The podium barely fit into the room. I had to move it to one side of the room or the other so that the entire class could see the board. It wasn't the best of conditions.

Plowing through the material, I gave them what they needed to know. I didn't ask any questions, nor did they. I was counting the minutes, as were they.

I was disappointed; more so at myself than at them.

Finally, I made it to the end of the semester. Finals. I don't like to give final exams. So, in an effort to be different, if not original, I require students to give a persuasive speech on the topic of his/her choice.

Every semester there is someone who delivers a speech that serves to open our eyes and hearts. And that semester was no exception.

The presentation that packed a punch was delivered by LaTanya, a twenty-four-year-old single mother of a five-year-old daughter.

She was a talkative young woman, always trying to get me to let class out early or prodding one of her classmates to go first. This day, she was egging her classmates to go before the class to deliver their speeches.

It was like pulling teeth; no one wanted to get it over with.

Tired of her smart remarks and wanting to move things along, I said, "Hey, you're trying to get everyone to go. Why don't you get up there?"

She cut me a look, grabbed large poster boards, and proceeded to the front to the room.

As LaTanya, placed the poster board, against the blackboard sill, she told the students she was going to persuade them not to become single parents.

To drive home her point, she made powerful use of those two large poster boards, each listing her expenses, everything from the monthly cost of her SUV to childcare, which totaled close to $3000 per month.

Although LaTanya earned $13.50 an hour working at a local factory, a good salary by most standards, she was left with little or no money at the end of the month.

The items listed didn't take into account any unforeseen

costs, like the dental work her daughter, who was recently in an accident, would now need.

She also informed students that it's not just about the money; she had to make other sacrifices as well. Serving as a role model for her daughter was important to LaTanya, so she had to forego late-night partying. Her good times were spent, not in a dark club dancing to loud music, but at her daughter's baton-twirling practices.

The students sat quietly as she spoke. No one looked away. No one dared comment. They were aghast at the real cost of raising a child. At its conclusion, her speech brought a round of applause and a few tears from the cocky class of eighteen to twenty-four-year-olds.

She sat down. I gave her a pat on the back.

"Good work," I said.

We heard many other speeches that day. The usual stuff — drinking and driving, cigarette smoking, and abortion.

None offered the heartfelt insights of LaTanya's. But just when things were beginning to become a bit mundane, something incredible happened.

One of the last remaining students to give a presentation stepped in front of the podium. She had in her hand a Bible which she placed on the table beside her.

The young brown-skinned woman wearing rumpled sweats, blue contacts, and looking a bit tired, proceeded to tell the audience that she was going to convince them of the importance of going to church.

As she began to talk, it was clear to all who were listening that she was unprepared. And although we didn't realize it at first, we, too, were clearly unprepared — unprepared for what were about to hear.

The young woman's speech turned into a rambling confession. She told how she was raised in the church but had not attended because she spent her nights partying. Tears streamed down her face as she told us that she had become pregnant at age fifteen and that she, now twenty, lives with her parents, who take the primary responsibility for raising her daughter.

She went on to say that her daughter just doesn't understand why she can't go out late at night with her mother. Heartbroken and missing her mommy, the little girl often cried herself to sleep.

The young woman said LaTanya's speech touched her. She admitted that her actions were wrong but she was unduly influenced by her peers. She promised to become a better mother for she, too, wanted her daughter's respect.

All this heartfelt honesty and humility came from a bold young woman who once wore a halter top to class and very tight sweatpants that said "Bootilicius" in glitter across the rear.

The students were once again uncharacteristically silent. And the tears flowed more freely than before. LaTanya was silent, head bowed throughout her peer's presentation.

The young woman went on for at least fifteen minutes, well past the seven-minute time limit. I dared not stop her. She needed to say it. And, in some way, we needed to hear it.

And we learned in that moment that LaTanya, in the very act of telling her truth, touched a heart, moved a soul. And we were all present to bear witness.

Finally, the young woman finished; she went back to her seat, sat down, and stared straight ahead.

I tapped LaTanya on the shoulder.

"You should talk to her after class," I whispered. She nodded.

The class ended. Everyone rushed out. I saw LaTanya follow the young woman.

I gathered my papers and caught up with LaTanya outside.

"Did you talk to her?" I asked.

"Yeah but she seemed like she didn't want to talk," said LaTanya, somewhat disappointed. "I told her if those girls were really her friends, they wouldn't ask her to go out knowing that her daughter needed her."

"You did good. Maybe she's just not ready to make a big change."

"You're right," she said slowly, walking away, finding some measure of comfort in knowing that she had planted the seeds for future change.

"Have a good summer," I said.

"You, too."

LaTanya should serve as an example for us all; for we should approach problems as if we are planting seeds not uprooting weeds.

Recently, I have read that, contrary to popular belief, adolescents want to know what their parents think, not just about sex, but about life in general, even if they don't like it and even if it's not very pretty. And they want the message to be specific — no beating around the bush, no using flowery euphemisms. I really think that's what we all want — someone to give it to us straight.

No one wants to hear from those who have not walked the same gravel-strewn path, barefoot and in pain, open wounds bleeding.

We want to know how those that came before made it through the fire, and we want those stories told with understanding, not self-righteousness or condemnation.

I learned something powerful: that all we can hope to do is change the world one person at a time. Heart to heart. Soul to soul. Confessing our own learned truths.

Epilogue

Where am I now?

Brooklyn, New York.

Nobody believed that I would leave Alabama.

I had every intention of leaving the moment I stepped my size eight-and-a-halfs on Alabama clay. When I shared my intention with my neighbors, co-workers, and friends, they'd laugh and say, "Right. You're not going anywhere." Or they would ask the most ridiculous of questions, "Why would you want to go to New York anyway?" And in response, I would give them a "Do you really need to ask?" look.

Oh yeah, I was leaving. I didn't know when or how and, to be honest, few people could really figure out why. No offers of lucrative positions could keep me. Not the clean air or the affordable housing. No, I wanted to go back to dirty smelly, crowded, surly New York City. Home. I knew what New York City was. I am not one to try to convince myself that sh**t doesn't stink.

And here I am . . . in Brooklyn.

Through a swirl of dead leaves and unknown debris that stings my eyes and adheres to my only shred of make-up — bright red lipstick, I trudge these streets — "incognegro." My presence, my existence is known only to me, the women at my Laundromat, the folks at Jamba Juice, the people at the bank, and the woman on the subway platform who turned out to be a colleague of mine from Brooklyn College.

After leading a life so filled with people, places, and experiences, I wanted anonymity — a word I can barely pronounce — allowing me time to think as I soak in the stench of subway air and feel some unknown sticky substance under my sneakers.

On a clear day when I can see two blocks down the street, I remember a time when I looked out at clear blue skies with billowing clouds, and I think about the people whom I called friends and Alabama, a place I find myself calling from time, to time "home."

Isn't that a kick in the head?